12/89

Twins in the

In the same series

A Mentally Handicapped Child in the Family
Mary McCormack

Caring for Elderly Parents
Eleanor Deeping

Families and Alcoholics
Alison Burr

Twins can be a great comfort to one another

Elizabeth M. Bryan

Twins in the family

Constable · London

First published in Great Britain 1984
by Constable and Company Limited
10 Orange Street, London WC2H 7EG
Copyright © 1984 by Elizabeth M. Bryan
Hardback ISBN 0 09 465560 x
Paperback ISBN 0 09 465570 7
Set in Lintron Baskerville 11 pt
by Rowland Phototypesetting Ltd
Bury St Edmunds, Suffolk
Printed in Great Britain by
St Edmundsbury Press
Bury St Edmunds, Suffolk

For my Grandmother

Preface

Ten years ago, as part of a medical research project on another subject I had the need, and the rare opportunity, of regularly seeing over one hundred mothers and their twins. I followed their progress throughout the first year and by the end I had become aware of a whole series of difficulties about the care of twins of which I had known little or nothing before.

I discovered that having twins was not always the unqualified joy that I, and so many others, had imagined. I was impressed not only by the practical, financial and emotional difficulties of looking after two babies at once but by the poor understanding and support these mothers received from family, friends or the caring professions. Most of them had been given little advice nor could they find any written information.

After discovering this situation the care of twins became my special interest. Apart from talking to more and more families with twins (I have now met several thousand), I helped a group of parents form a 'Parents of Twins' club in York and in 1978 I was involved in the formation of the national Twins Clubs Association.

Having written a book for doctors I realised that, although several useful books on the general care of twins had appeared in recent years, there might also be a need for one which concentrated on the special difficulties encountered by some parents.

For many years it was precisely their problems, not their

joys, that most parents of twins most wanted to talk to me about. Gradually I accumulated a useful if somewhat daunting collection of difficulties and dilemmas, most of them via personal meetings but many through extensive correspondence. I am deeply grateful to all the parents who have shared their problems with me over the years.

I have quoted from many of the helpful letters from parents that I have been privileged to see as President of the T.C.A. but have preserved the necessary confidentiality by altering names and other details in each case.

It is to the conscientiousness, caring and the practical experiences of the parents themselves that I have been most indebted in writing this book.

October 1983

Acknowledgements

Ideally I would name every one of the many hundreds of parents, mothers and fathers, who have shared with me so generously over the years their fund of experience in caring for twins. I must however give particular thanks to those who gave me detailed criticisms of the manuscript itself, Barbara Broadbent, Charlene France, Trevor and Caroline Oddy, Marie Oxtoby, Ros Peter, Emlyn and Sara Roberts, Susan Scorer, Lesley Skinner, Linda Smither and Rosemary and Keith Thompson.

Many members of the committee of the Twins Clubs Association helped in a variety of ways and I am especially grateful to Judi Linney and Dee Hoseason.

I am of course myself responsible for the opinions expressed.

I am indebted to Eve Vinten for helping me keep contact with so many families and to Jane Gardiner and Wendy Spicer for typing the manuscript.

Without the constant help of my husband, Ronald Higgins, not least his literary skills, I might never have undertaken the task.

I would like to thank Judi Linney for Fig. 1–3; Dr Valerie Farr for Fig. 3–1; M. G. Bulmer and The Clarendon Press for Fig. 2–1; Joan Moore who drew Figs. 4–1, 4–2 and 5–5 first reproduced by Baillière Tindall Ltd.: Gordon Taylor for photography for the frontispiece, Figs. 9–4 and 10–3.

I have dedicated the book to my grandmother, Violet Hoyle,

now in her 97th year, in gratitude for the love, encouragement and baked custards which have sustained me for as long as I can remember, not least in the years in which I first became absorbed in the subject of this book.

EMB

Contents

Illustrations

Illustrations

[1]

Introduction

People are fascinated by twins – as every parent discovers. This fascination has deep psychological roots. In the first place it is a marvel of nature that two babies can be conceived together and born together. But also it can intrigue us, believing as we do in the uniqueness of each human individual, that some of us can have an identical copy. These notions are expressed in mythology and tribal customs, but so is the idea of a special relationship between twins both identical and fraternal, which is often one of conflict.

Twins have excited much interest since biblical times and before. The most famous pair of twin-rivals was Esau and Jacob, conceived as a result of Isaac's prayer for his barren wife, Rebekah. The conflict between them was said to have started within the womb, a struggle for the birthright. Esau won this round but finally lost when Jacob tricked his father into giving him the elder son's blessing.

Another pair of twins described in Genesis are Pharez and Zarah, the children of Tamar and Judah. They too competed to be delivered first. Zarah presented an arm in the birth canal which was labelled with red string. Later when the babies were born the string was attached to the second baby showing that Pharez had replaced Zarah in birth order.

The only twin mentioned in the New Testament is Thomas, the apostle. His name is in fact derived from the Hebrew word for twin, 'te-om'.

Twins in the family

In Greek and Roman mythology twins abound. Many were gods or the offspring of gods and as such had supernatural powers. Castor and Pollux, the twin sons of Leda by Tyndareus and Zeus, had powers over the wind and waves and became known as the seafarers' guardians. When Castor was killed in battle, Pollux was so desolate that he begged his father, Zeus, to allow him to join his brother. They became the heavenly constellation, Gemini, meaning twins.

In Roman mythology Romulus and Remus are the most famous twins. They were the sons of Mars and one of the Vestal Virgins, Silvia. The babies were supposed to be drowned with their mother in the River Tiber but their cradle reached the bank where they were found and suckled by a she-wolf. There are statues depicting them with her in both Rome and Siena. (Figure 1/1) When they grew up the two brothers wanted to found a great city but could not agree on a site. In their dispute Romulus killed Remus and went on to found the city of Rome over which he ruled for many years.

Narcissus, from whom the derogatory term 'narcissism' or self-worship is derived, was also, according to one source, a twin, though much maligned. Narcissus had a twin sister to whom he was devoted. It was only after she died that he spent long hours looking at his own reflection in a pool. This was not out of vanity, but to remind himself of his lost sister.

Motifs of twins are often seen amongst the gods of the Asiatic religions. Sometimes these are depicted as 'Siamese twins' – a figure with two heads or one with several sets of limbs. The Ashvins are twin gods in Indian mythology and are believed to look after the weak and oppressed.

In Mexico the ancient Aztecs worshipped the goddess of fertility, Xochiquetzal, who they believed to be the first mother of twins.

Throughout history there have been strongly held cultural and religious beliefs about twins in most parts of the world. Many of these persist today though usually in modified and less

18

1/1 Statue of Romulus and Remus being suckled by a she-wolf

extreme forms. Within the last twenty years an English paediatrician working in Zimbabwe was upset to find that after a pair of premature twins had been successfully nursed in hospital under his care for several months, one was killed on the day the babies were due to return to their own village. It was the custom of the tribe to kill twins.

Attitudes to twins can vary greatly even between different tribes living quite close to each other. For some twins the difference between being born on one side of the river rather than the other may be that between being welcomed, even worshipped, and being rejected and killed.

The killing of twins used to be widespread. It has been

reported from many parts of Africa and Asia as well as amongst Australian Aborigines and the Eskimos. There are various explanations as to why twins should be so intensely disliked, even feared. One is that it is animal-like for a human mother to have more than one baby at a time. Another is that two babies must mean two fathers: the mother must therefore have either committed adultery or have conceived the second baby through an evil spirit. It is not for comfortably living Europeans to offer simplistic condemnations of these customs. There can often be a practical side to them, they serve a social function. In a nomadic tribe it is difficult for a mother to carry two babies for many miles, and when food is scarce breast-feeding two babies may be simply impossible. Both could die where one twin might have survived. Some tribes killed both babies, some just the second-born or, in boy/girl pairs, the girl.

In other tribes only boy/girl pairs were killed. They were condemned because of the fear of incest, not least during the nine months of intimacy in the womb! On the other hand the Bantu positively welcomed boy/girl pairs, regarding them as newly-weds. In parts of Japan and the Philippines such pairs were later expected to marry.

Mothers of twins were often condemned with their twins. The Ibo tribe considered giving birth to twins as one of the five great sins against the fertility goddess, Ala, together with kidnapping, poisoning, stealing and committing adultery! So great can be the fear of twins that one tribe had a ritual wedding prayer which asked that the couple's 'house might be filled with children *one by one*'.

'May you become the mother of twins' was in some West African tribes the strongest curse. Sometimes words were unnecessary: two fingers of the right hand pointed towards a woman could have the same terrible effect. Similarly in one tribal language there was no graver insult than to say a man was the type who would have intercourse with the mother of twins. In some areas, this was a crime punishable by death.

In some tribes mothers were killed together with their babies or others were banished to the bush where they were destined to remain, sometimes for life, in communities known as 'twin towns'. When the presence of a second baby was discovered in the Ibo tribe the mother was sometimes moved from the village, still in labour, so that she would not contaminate the area. When a second baby was born unexpectedly elaborate rituals of purification of the whole village were performed. All unused food and half burnt firewood was thrown out.

On the whole, fathers of twins were let off lightly. Some North American Indians insisted on a period of abstinence from meat and fish which must have been hard for a hunter. In parts of Peru the father had to abstain from salt, pepper and sexual intercourse for six months – an intriguing trio.

After this litany of customs and traditions hostile to twins I should stress that other tribes welcome them and greatly respect the mother. Special ceremonies are performed and songs sung in her honour. Special food is prepared and the best vegetables are saved for her. The Cocopas in North America believe that twins come down from heaven and must be treated with great care and respect lest they be tempted to return to their heavenly home.

In some parts of the world there are elaborate ceremonies associated with twins. They figure particularly in the Ibeji cult of the Nigerian Yoruba tribe. Ibeji literally means 'to beget two' and through the traffic of slaves the Ibeji cult has spread to many parts of South and Central America and the Caribbean.

Carved wooden images (Figure 1/2), sometimes in large numbers, are used for special rituals and are kept in places of worship to the goddess of twins. There is a temple in Nigeria dedicated to this goddess to which a mother and her twins make a pilgrimage as soon as the children are able to walk.

Twins are often believed to have supernatural powers, both good and bad, over the weather. The Egyptian twin gods, Shu and Tefnut, were respectively the wind god and rain god. The

similar powers of Castor and Pollux have already been mentioned.

In parts of Western and Southern Africa twins were thought
to cause famine due to drought or flood and were therefore
killed at birth to prevent such a catastrophe.

Many North American Indians also held twins responsible
for the climatic conditions. The Mohaves, for instance, believed
that twins came from the sky and used lightning, thunder and
rain as their means of descent. The Tsimshian, when praying
for a storm to abate, would say 'calm down breath of twins'.
Many South American Indian tribes also attributed aspects of
the weather to the mood and behaviour of their twins. Indeed
twins were used to forecast the weather according to their state
of health. When the twins were feeling well the weather should
be clement, when they had a headache or indigestion a storm
was likely.

Twins in many African tribes are given fixed traditional
names. Amongst the Yoruba the first-born twin is called Taiwo
(he who has the first taste of the world) and the second is
Kainde or Kehinde (he who lags behind). I well remember
meeting a Taiwo and Kainde for the first time when a Nigerian
mother brought her six-month-old twin daughters to my clinic
for their immunisations. They had several pairs of twin cousins
called, of course, Taiwo and Kainde. That would be confusing
enough but at least they were not facing the greater confusion,
not uncommon in Nigeria, of a second or third pair of twins
with the same names as their brothers and sisters.

Amongst the Bantu, boy twins are called Aburi and Nobese
and the girls, Abuda and Tandabo. In various other parts of
Africa twins are called Ochin and Omo, Tali and Bali, Buth
and Duoth. In Dahomey the children following twins also have
special names. The first is Dosu, then comes Dosa and then
Donyo.

For couples longing to have twins there has never been a
shortage of prescriptions! In medieval Scotland, a tumbler full

1/2 Wooden twin images from West Africa, linked by a chain. The
 whole is made from one piece of wood

of water from the well in St Mungo ensured a twin birth. In
parts of the Far East today a double banana, chestnut or millet
seed added to the diet of a mother is confidently believed to
cause twins.

Some North American Indians say that twins occur if the
mother lies on her back instead of on her side in labour, so that
the baby splits into two. Others believe that too much work
during pregnancy can result in twins. The Mundugumor in
New Guinea believed that twins might result if a husband had
intercourse with his wife when she was pregnant.

In some traditions twins themselves are thought to be able to
induce fertility in others. In Wales they were invited to wed-
dings to ensure children for the newly-weds. Twins are evidence of high fertility in the mother and some tribes believe this
fertility can be transferred to the land. Mothers of twins may be
required to join elaborate rituals to ensure a good harvest.

It has often been believed that a twin would rarely survive the death of the other and if a twin does survive he is thought likely to be exceptionally strong, possessing the vitality of both.

In Sussex it was thought that a single surviving twin had special healing powers, that he or she could cure the fungal infection thrush for example, by breathing into the mouth of the sufferer.

Surviving twins in Africa may often carry a wooden image representing their dead twin around their neck or waist. This gives company to the survivor and a refuge for the spirit of the dead. The image has to be cared for as his twin. The mother must oil and dress the figure and offer it token food. When the survivor is old enough he is expected to care for his twin himself.

Some of these beliefs and superstitions may seem strange and irrational to us but, as I have suggested, they often make more sense in particular local conditions. Even in the most scientifically advanced societies, moreover, there are still many aspects of twinning and its origins that remain a mystery.

It has been known for centuries that there are two types of twins – identical twins who are very similar in looks and fraternal twins who look no more alike than any other brother or sister.

The true origin of these different types, however, was not understood. In the sixteenth century it was even thought possible for a boy and girl pair of twins to be 'identical', as shown by the amusing confusion between Viola and her brother Sebastian in *Twelfth Night*, when Shakespeare says 'an apple cleft in twain is not more twin than these two creatures.'

We now know that identical twins arise when a normal fertilised ovum (egg) divides into two and each of the halves become a separate individual but each with the same genes (Figure 1/3). This is why identical twins are otherwise known as uniovular (one ovum), monozygous or monozygotic (one zygote). A zygote is a fertilised ovum. Identical twins always, therefore, have the same basic physical features such as eye and

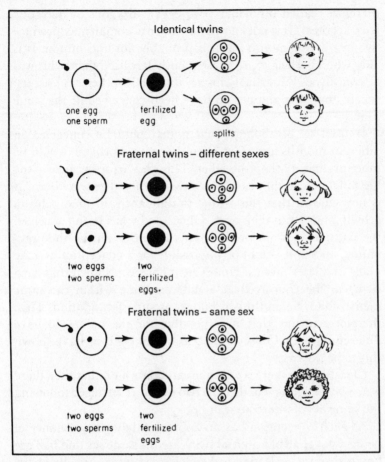

1/3 The origins of the two types of twins

hair colour and bone structure. They will not, however, necessarily be indistinguishable. Environmental influences, particularly nourishment, can greatly affect their looks, and their nourishment can even be different before they are born, as will be seen later.

Fraternal twins, otherwise known as non-identical, occur when two ova are fertilised in one menstrual cycle. They are,

25

therefore, called binovular (two eggs), dizygous or dizygotic (two zygotes). It is not known how often a woman may produce two ova in one month but it is probably not uncommon. It is only when both eggs are subsequently fertilised that twins will be conceived. Fraternal twins are thus like brothers and sisters, except that they happen to have been conceived at the same time.

It used to be thought that twins could be conceived in different months and thus when they were born one would be more premature than the other. This idea arose because of the big difference in the size of some twins when they were born. It is now known that this is due to differences in their rates of growth and not in their ages. Once a baby has been conceived the mother does not produce any more ova during the pregnancy, and so it would be impossible for a conception to take place in a later month. However, it has been shown that each twin can be conceived at a different time within the same menstrual cycle and this is known as superfecundation. This, therefore, means that it is possible for the babies to have different fathers. On several occasions blood tests have shown this to be the case.

Clearly when there is only one candidate for father then there is no way of telling whether the two ova were fertilised following the same act of intercourse or not.

As each conception has an approximately 50–50 chance of being a boy, half of fraternal twins are the same sex and half are boy/girl pairs. (All identical twins must, of course, be of the same sex.)

It is theoretically possible for there to be a third type of twin which would arise if a single ovum divided and then two sperms each fertilised one of the two halves. It is likely that this does occasionally happen but it has yet to be conclusively proven.

In England and Wales there are approximately six thousand pairs of twins born each year. Of these, two-thirds are fraternal and one-third identical. Of the total, therefore, about one-third will be boy/girl pairs, a third will be both girls and a third will be both boys.

Amongst single children there are slightly fewer girls than boys born, whereas with twins the sexes are about equally distributed. Indeed just recently girl twins have outnumbered boy twins. The reason for this difference is not known.

In the 1950s the incidence of twins in the United Kingdom was about one in eighty deliveries but over the past 30 years the rate has gradually fallen and is now about one in every hundred. During the past five years the incidence has remained steady and it may not decline any further.

News of the Twins

The first person to suspect that twins are on the way is often a mother herself. This was certainly so before ultrasound scanning came into common use.

Expectant mothers have told me of all sorts of clues that first made them wonder whether they might be having more than one baby. One said, 'I had to go into maternity clothes by three months,' and one laughed saying, 'It felt like a football scrum inside.' Yet another reported, 'It was like having an octopus for a baby – there seemed to be so many arms and legs.'

Not uncommonly, however, twins fool both their mothers and the obstetricians. In some hospitals as many as one in seven births of twins are not suspected until after the first baby has arrived. I well remember one midwife's (and father's) expression of amazement, if not horror, when a baby girl popped out instead of the placenta (after birth). Another mother found that her so-called fibroid turned out to be a second baby. Fortunately these surprises are becoming less common, in the developed world at least, as more hospitals introduce routine screening with ultrasound scans and alphafetoprotein (AFP) blood testing.

A twin pregnancy can now be detected as early as six weeks by ultrasound scan. These scans are not foolproof however. I have known several mothers who have had scans and the second baby was still missed. The most common cause for this is that one baby is hidden behind the other in the womb.

AFP is a protein produced by the fetus which crosses the placenta into the mother's blood circulation. Measurements on a small sample of blood from the mother, are usually made to detect babies with spina bifida or similar abnormalities as they tend to have a high level of AFP. However, a high level may also be the first hint of twins. Two babies produce twice as much of this protein and so mothers carrying twins often show high levels. It is only when an ultrasound scan shows twins that a mother can be reassured that the high level of AFP in her blood means nothing worse! One mother wrote, 'I had a test carried out at 3½ months which showed some abnormality in my blood protein but two weeks later the "abnormality" proved to be twins. The other possibilities are too horrible to think about.' A number of parents have a period of intense anxiety awaiting the final results.

Lastly, but not least, it may be the obstetrician or midwife who first suspect a multiple pregnancy. They may feel a second head or extra limbs. They may hear two distinct heart beats. Or the size of the womb may not agree with the mother's dates.

The news

Doctors and midwives sometimes forget how momentous the news of a double pregnancy can be to those actually responsible for it and for its enduring consequences! I have heard horrifying tales of the indirect, even casual, way in which mothers were told. Some just happened to overhear it. Similarly parents may have unnecessary anxiety if they realise that their scan is causing interest but are not immediately told about the twins. One mother who knew that her scan was under special scrutiny thought that her baby must be grossly deformed.

The earlier the diagnosis is made the longer parents have to make all the practical preparations. They may need to order a second set of equipment; to double the pile of nappies; to find yet more recruits for the knitting army. All these are important. But just as important, if not more so, is the time for emotional preparation.

For nearly all parents the news of twins is a shock – even if often a welcome one. Let me quote some phrases I have heard used: flabbergasted but happy and excited ... also very anxious; over the moon; suffering from shell shock; dazed and apprehensive; totally overwhelmed, wondering how I shall cope; thrilled but feeling very ignorant and helpless. It must help if parents are enabled to work through these immediate reactions and, so far as possible, come to terms with them before the babies arrive.

For the mother who already feels a deep loving bond with the baby in her womb it can be very disturbing, ('eerie' as one mother described it) to find that this single love must suddenly turn into two. It may take several weeks to adjust, to accept fully the extra unexpected baby. The mother who has plenty of warning is likely to find it very much easier to relate to both babies.

Reactions

Reactions plainly vary greatly. But how do most parents respond to the news? Nearly all admit it is a shock – despite whatever suspicions they may have had. Even the history of ten sets of twins in the family failed to prepare one mother for the news!

Soon after the shock, or along with it, comes joy. Or so it does for many mothers. There is particular joy at the prospect of a second child if a mother has had difficulty in conceiving. Many parents are pleased to have two children for the price of one pregnancy. Some are just delighted to have twins as such – the dream apparently of many mothers.

Most mothers who are expecting their first baby are thrilled if it turns out to be two. For other mothers it may be a question of fatalistic acceptance. But for some the news comes as a really cruel blow. Perhaps the pregnancy itself was unplanned. Maybe the cost of an extra baby could strain an already precarious family budget, or even be the last straw in breaking a tottering marriage. Maybe the mother is alone and, while being prepared to cope with one child, is overwhelmed by the thought of two.

For well over half the families the arrival of twins means that the family has at least one more child than was originally intended. For many this whole pregnancy was an 'accident'. The most likely (and often the least eager) to have twins appear in fact to be elderly mothers, those who already have large families, single mothers and those who conceive in the first three months of marriage.

On the whole fathers are more generally welcoming than mothers to the news of twins. One mother wrote, 'My husband is thrilled to bits but all I can see are difficulties and problems.' Perhaps this is because fathers tend to be less aware of the practical and emotional implications. Of twenty-three fathers I interviewed on the subject all but one said they were delighted by the news. The twenty-third father, who had claimed to be dismayed, was then heard boasting in the pub of his achievement! Little do most men realise, or admit if they do, that all credit for twins rests with the mother (see p. 33).

Questions

Whether thrilled or dismayed, or a bit of both, all parents wonder why it has happened and what lies ahead. These questions are often difficult to present at first. The manner of doctors in a hectic antenatal clinic often seems to have the effect of freezing the thoughts of mothers. Even the most articulate parents can feel lost for words.

It is vital that parents should have the chance – and the determination – to ask questions and voice their fears as they arise. A written list of questions can be a useful *aide-mémoire*. Too often small worries become huge fears which usually turn out to be quite unfounded. One father, a farmer I later got to know well in Yorkshire, had a boy and girl twin and had worried unnecessarily for nine months that his little girl would never be able to have children. He finally plucked up courage to ask a doctor about this. His relief, when he heard that human twins are not the same as their bovine counterparts, was enormous. Female calves are affected by masculinising hormones which cross the placenta from their male twin. They then grow up sterile and are known as freemartins. In humans there is no link between the placentas.

Another mother showed me her pretty four-year-old identical twin girls and asked whether I could tell which one of them would be unable to have children. Since the twins were born she had been under the misapprehension, which I have since discovered that others share, that one girl of an identical pair is bound to be infertile.

There are endless old wives' tales about twins. Some originate from the superstitions discussed in Chapter 1. People love to regale expectant parents with them. Beware!

But on to the questions that parents ask. 'Why us?' is usually the first and is the hardest to answer. We still have little idea about the causes of twinning. We know how twins happen but not why. The exceptions are those women who took 'fertility' drugs to help them to conceive. Such women should have been warned that the chance of them having twins (or triplets or more) is increased, although not nearly as much now that doctors have learned to better regulate the dosage.

Every woman seems to have an equal chance of having identical twins whatever her age, race or size and whether or not there are twins in the family. Why the occasional fertilised ovum (egg) should split into two is still a mystery. Identical twins have very occasionally been reported to run in a family. This happens so rarely as to be of no significance to the general population (although it certainly is to a particular family! see page 177).

Fraternal twins are a different matter. We know that certain groups of women are more likely to have two ova fertilised in the same month. Fraternal twins are most common in Negro and least in Mongolian races. The twinning rate amongst Europeans, North Americans, and Indians lies somewhere in between. The incidence of twinning increases with the age of the mother, reaching a peak between the ages of thirty-five and thirty-nine, and also with her parity (the number of her previous children) (Figure 2/1). Nutrition is another factor and tall women are more prone to twins than small. It therefore follows that a tall, older African mother with several children, is much more likely to have twins than a small, young Japanese woman expecting her first baby.

Thus we know some of the factors that influence fraternal twinning or are at least associated with it. These factors are probably all related to the level of fertility of the mother. The more easily you conceive the more likely you are to have twins. Single mothers (and those who conceive quickly after marriage) have a high rate of twinning presumably because they are a highly fertile group – many run the risk but it is the more fertile who are likely to 'fall'!

Susan's story is an example. She became pregnant at seventeen. Within four years she had twins and three single children. She decided that was enough but an 'accident' occurred when the first two were eleven. This turned out to be undiagnosed twins, a boy and a girl. Luckily she loved children, breast-fed the lot and took it all in her stride. Others might be more perturbed by their high fertility.

Fraternal twins do run in families but only through the mother. So, however many twins the father has in his family this will have no effect on his chances of having twin children.

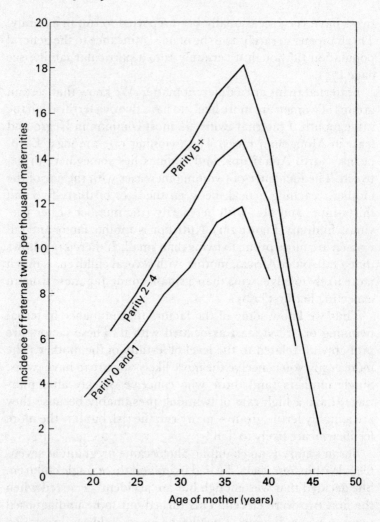

2/1 Graph showing the incidence of fraternal twins in relation to the mother's age and parity

This odd fact is rarely realised, even by doctors, let alone insurance brokers!

We are still however far from being able to predict whether a particular woman will have twins or even to give her the odds against.

What lies ahead?

Even with a straightforward single pregnancy many mothers have questions and some have fears. All such mothers, however, will know others who have been through the same experiences to whom they can turn. Dozens of people will positively deluge the expectant mother with advice and detailed accounts of their own experiences. With a multiple pregnancy it is different. I find that most mothers when they are first told to expect two babies, don't know any other family with young twins.

Voices of experience are usually hard to find. The most many mothers get is a torrent of old wives' tales. At best these are confusing. At worst they are dangerously misleading.

All mothers are anxious to know what lies ahead. Will the pregnancy be more difficult? Are the babies likely to be small and frail? How can I feed two, nurse two, love two, at the same time? What about equipment, dressing, transport, reactions of the rest of the family? The questions are endless. Who can reply?

Meeting someone else who has been through it all can be not only helpful but deeply reassuring.

Local 'Mothers of Twins' clubs can fulfil this vital role. There are about 150 such clubs throughout the UK. There are many more in the United States, Canada, South Africa, Australia, Japan, France, Holland and New Zealand. These are self-help groups who support and advise mothers of twins and offer the important opportunity of sharing their special problems and experiences. The groups also serve highly practical purposes such as the exchange of secondhand clothes and equipment. The clubs will welcome new members from the moment the twins are diagnosed (*see* Chapter 7).

The national Twins Clubs Association (*see* Appendix) has a list of all local clubs in the United Kingdom.

[3]

Waiting

Mothers who get only a few weeks or days warning of twins have little time to adjust or prepare. Others, whose second baby was detected early, will have time to reflect, to plan and to learn about what lies ahead both for themselves and their partner.

What sort of questions do mothers ask?

Is a twin pregnancy any different from a single pregnancy? Will it feel different? Are there more likely to be complications? Are special precautions necessary? How does a twin baby grow and develop compared with a single baby?

For many mothers a twin pregnancy does not feel obviously different from a single one and that is why so many twin pregnancies went undetected in the past. On the whole a twin pregnancy is the same as a single one but discomforts and complications tend to be increased.

Problems

A few mothers suffer quite severe sickness during the first three months. This is probably due to the high level of hormones circulating through the body.

The bulk as well as the weight of the extra baby means that a mother is likely to have more general discomfort. She may get more indigestion and 'heartburn' and may be able to eat only small snacks at a time. Backache may be troublesome and general mobility difficult, which can become very disheartening. Many mothers, for example, are unable to get in and out of the bath during the last few weeks. Lying flat is often uncomfortable and support with a bolster or several firm pillows can be helpful. These discomforts can be very distressing but at least they do not affect the babies.

A particularly close eye is kept on all mothers with twins during the last three months or so of the pregnancy. This is partly so that premature labour can be detected early and, sometimes, even prevented (*see* page 50), and partly because there are certain complications which are rather more common with twins. These complications can harm the babies (and the mother) if they are not recognised and treated promptly.

Some mothers, especially those in their first pregnancy, get a high blood pressure together with swelling of their hands and feet and/or protein in the urine. This condition is known as pre-eclamptic toxaemia. Toxaemia is more common in twin pregnancies and should it occur the mother will be advised to rest in bed, probably in hospital.

Polyhydramnios – a condition in which excess fluid accumulates around the fetus – is more common in twins (but still rare) and can be very uncomfortable. The mother may notice her abdomen suddenly enlarging much faster than before. Sometimes it appears for no apparent reason and the babies are undisturbed by it. At other times it may be a sign that all is not well with one or both babies and that it would be safer if they were delivered. The doctors will make a careful check of all mothers with polyhydramnios.

Because the mother is supporting two babies she will need extra food and in particular iron to prevent anaemia. She will usually be given iron tablets throughout her pregnancy and her haemoglobin level will be checked regularly in the antenatal clinic.

Is it safe to make love during the pregnancy? Most couples ask themselves this question but unfortunately many are too embarrassed to ask their obstetrician. For some women sexual intercourse is safe and enjoyable throughout the pregnancy. For others it is physically too awkward during the last few weeks.

Some couples need to be cautious at certain times. Those who have had previous miscarriages are often advised to abstain from sexual intercourse during the first three months of pregnancy. It is not the insertion of the penis into the vagina that provokes a miscarriage but rather the contractions of the womb that accompany a woman's orgasm. For the same reason a mother who is likely to go into premature labour is wise to abstain in the later months.

The obstetrician is always the best person to give advice and couples should not hesitate to ask.

Amniocentesis

One of the most useful procedures that has been developed recently in antenatal care is that of testing the fluid surrounding the developing baby, to identify certain possible abnormalities. This is known as amniocentesis. Its greatest use is in the detection of Down's Syndrome (mongolism), and, as the chances of having a baby with this condition increase with the age of a mother, there are many units who offer the test to all older mothers. Many mothers welcome the chance to have the test and would choose to have the pregnancy terminated if the baby was found to be abnormal.

But parents of twins are faced with a dilemma. The chances of both babies being abnormal are relatively small. What would they do if they found they had one abnormal and one normal child? Many parents who would not hesitate to have a pregnancy terminated for a single abnormal baby could not agree if it meant sacrificing a normal baby at the same time. Yet the stress of knowing that she is carrying an abnormal baby for the remainder of the pregnancy may have a terrible effect on a mother.

For others the decision whether to have the pregnancy terminated or not may depend on whether the affected child is likely to die at, or soon after, birth or whether he would survive as a burden to himself, to his twin and to his family.

It is technically more difficult to perform an amniocentesis in a multiple pregnancy and some parents are faced with the problem of making a decision on the results from only one baby. There is also a slightly greater risk of inducing a miscarriage. For these reasons, as well as the risk of an agonising choice discussed earlier, some obstetricians feel than an amniocentesis should not be carried out in a twin pregnancy.

It is now possible to kill the abnormal baby whilst still in the womb and allow the healthy twin to develop as a normal single baby, but it will be a long time before this option is generally available and, even when it is, parents will need to give deep thought as to whether they can cope with the emotional strain of knowing the dead baby is still in the womb for the rest of the pregnancy. Before making any of these decisions it is always helpful to talk to other parents who have been faced with the same dilemma. Contact can often be made either through your obstetrician or through the Twins Clubs Association.

Miscarriage

Some mothers fear that they will lose their twins by a miscarriage, or spontaneous abortion as it is technically termed. In practice a miscarriage in a twin pregnancy is little more common than in a single one but when it does happen identical twins seem to be at a greater risk than fraternal. This is probably due to the complications that can arise when two babies share the same placenta and blood circulation: one baby may receive an unfair share of the blood supply.

However, miscarrying one of the two babies may happen much more often than we realise. It seems that half, if not more, of mothers who conceive twins end up with only one baby. Most will never even know that they conceived twins. It is only since the advent of ultrasound scans in early pregnancy that these 'vanishing twins' have been recognised. Some mothers have no signs when one baby dies. Others may think they have had a complete miscarriage and then to their surprise, and usually pleasure, they discover that they are still pregnant.

By the time the single baby is born there is usually no sign that there has been another fetus, although an ultrasound scan during the pregnancy may reveal an empty sac where the fetus has died. If a twin dies after the first three months it is rarely miscarried but instead shrivels up and can be seen attached to the placenta. It is then called a fetus papyraceus.

Coping with these sorts of experience is very distressing and I return to this subject in Chapter 14.

The normal fetus

Over the past ten years an increasing number of maternity units are using ultrasound scans. A scan can reveal whether there is more than one baby and repeated scans will show how the baby/babies is/are growing (Figure 3/1).

Some maternity units now scan all pregnant women routinely at the end of the first three months to identify any with twins. Others will only scan if a mother is uncertain of her dates or if twins are suspected. Although twins can be detected as early as six weeks ultrasound scans are rarely done as early as this.

Most units are happy to have the father present during the scan, and he and the mother should be able to watch the screen during the procedure. A helpful radiographer will explain what is being shown – sometimes both babies' heads and various

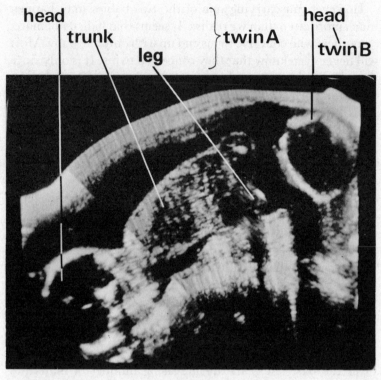

head
trunk
leg
} twin A
head
twin B

3/1 Ultrasound scan of twin pregnancy at 24 weeks

parts of the bodies are distinguishable. At other times one baby may be completely hidden behind the other.

Some over-enthusiastic radiographers try to interpret more than is possible from a scan. They may unintentionally mislead parents by telling them whether or not their twins are identical. For instance, many mothers have been firmly told that the twins will not be identical on the grounds that there are two separate placentas. This does not necessarily follow, as we will see in the next chapter. Likewise it is difficult, often impossible, to identify the membranes of the placenta on a scan and so a single chorion placenta (which always belongs to identical twins) cannot safely be distinguished from a fused double chorion placenta. Parents who initially would not have minded one way or the other can be quite disconcerted if they find the twins are very different when they had adjusted to the idea of having identical twins or vice versa.

Growth of the babies

Ultrasound scans are often repeated several times during the pregnancy because this is a good way of checking on how the babies are growing. There are several ways of measuring the growth of the baby on the ultrasound scan and the most commonly used is the biparietal diameter (the side to side diameter of the baby's head). The rate of growth of a baby's head is a good indication of its whole body growth. Some obstetricians find that other measurements, such as the length from head to tail (crown-rump length) are equally useful.

One of the problems in a twin pregnancy is that of following the progress of each baby individually. If one is growing satisfactorily then there may be no indication that the other is doing less well. There may be no signs on examining a mother or on checking her hormone levels to suggest that the second baby is in trouble. This is why ultrasound is especially useful in twin pregnancies because each baby can be studied separately. It is not unusual to find that twins who have been growing at the same speed during the first half of the pregnancy diverge later, and this is a sign that the smaller baby is not getting as much nourishment. If his growth remains slow on successive ultrasound scans then the obstetrician may decide to deliver the babies early in order to save the little one.

Newborn twins are on average two pounds lighter than single babies. This is partly because they tend to be born early. But even those who have lasted to full term are a pound or so lighter.

Of course there are always exceptions and I have seen a number of pairs of bouncing eight pounders!

On the whole, however, a mother cannot nourish two babies as satisfactorily as one right through to the end of the pregnancy. Up to about 26 weeks, that is the first six months, twin babies seem to grow just as well as single ones. Presumably the placenta is able to provide enough nourishment until then. After that the weight of twins increases more slowly than single babies and so the weight difference between them gets larger as the pregnancy continues.

Identical twins are, on average, slightly smaller than fraternal. This is not just because they may be born more prematurely. The full explanation is not clear but there have been several reasons suggested. It may be because most of them have to share the same blood circulation and thus some of the nourishment is wasted. It may be because they have started from one egg instead of two. Or it may be because fraternal twins tend to have taller mothers and size is to some extent inherited.

Abnormalities

Many mothers expecting twins are fearful that something will be wrong with the babies just because they are twins. This is a natural fear but there are really no good grounds for it. Twins are little, if any, more likely to be born with an abnormality than single babies. Certainly this is so with fraternal twins. In fact there are some conditions that are actually less common amongst twins – Down's Syndrome for example. Identical twins do have a slightly higher risk but, even with identical twins, if one baby is abnormal the other one is often quite healthy.

Siamese twins were named after the famous brothers from Siam, Chang and Eng. They were joined together by a small

3/2 Chang and Eng, Siamese twins, with their wives and some of
       their 22 children

band of tissue between their chests. Chang and Eng lived full
and active lives. They married sisters and had twenty-two
children between them (Figure 3/2).
   One of the most famous English pairs was Eliza and Mary
Chulkhurst from Kent who are illustrated on the village sign,

45

the Biddenden Maids. Born in 1100, they were joined at the shoulders and hips (Figure 3/3). They were great benefactresses to the village and when they died the Chulkhurst Charity was established and part of this includes the distribution each Easter of biscuits decorated with their picture.

Siamese, or conjoined, twins are very rare. Because of their rarity it is difficult to give an exact incidence but it seems to be in the order of one in a thousand pairs of twins. They occur when the fertilised egg splits late in development and these twins will always be identical. Nowadays quite a number can be successfully separated with the healthy survival of both twins.

3/3 The Chulkhurst sisters born in the year
1100, who lived to the age of 34 and died
within six hours of each other

Monoamniotic Twins

Most twins are separated from each other in the womb by at least one membrane (the amnion). Occasionally both twins are contained in the same sac and they are then known as mono-amniotic twins (Figure 4/2). They will swim about together all through the pregnancy and, not surprisingly, sometimes get entangled in each other's umbilical cords, which link the babies to the placenta. However, more often than not the twins are unaffected by this and, unless the placenta is carefully ex-amined or the cords are actually knotted, it may not even be noticed that these were in fact monoamniotic twins.

Monoamniotic twins are always identical and the fact that both fetuses share an amniotic sac means that the fertilised ovum must have divided relatively late, that is after the amnion was already developed.

Chimera

Most people have a single blood group. Occasionally, however, a fraternal twin may have blood cells of two different groups. This only happens if blood has crossed from one twin to the other before they are born. When it does happen it does no harm and is usually just discovered by chance when a blood test is being done for some quite different reason. This condition is known as chimerism and is very rare.

[4]
Birth

In this country mothers of twins are almost always delivered in hospital. The rare exceptions are those mothers who have chosen to have a home delivery of a single baby and are surprised by the arrival of a second; or mothers who are caught short by the extremely rapid delivery of some premature twins and, thirdly, the few mothers who insist, misguidedly in my view, on having their twins at home.

There are, of course, several arguments in favour of a home delivery for single babies – for twins there are none. The risks are too high. Firstly, twins are much more likely to be premature and therefore in need of special care. Secondly, there are various complications which can be avoided or treated in hospital but could be a danger to both mother and babies at home. For instance the second baby may present awkwardly so that forceps are needed and possibly an anaesthetic.

'When will I go into labour?' is the question that all pregnant mothers would like to have answered. This is not just to make practical planning easier – and for father to book time off work – but also to save the daily suspense as the 'expected date of delivery' draws nearer. At least with a single pregnancy there is a strong chance that this will occur in the three weeks or so after the 38th week.

Twin pregnancies are far less predictable. Although the average length for a twin pregnancy is 37 weeks about one in three mothers will deliver earlier than this and some will go right through to 40 weeks. At present it is difficult to predict for a particular mother. One problem is that we don't know just what triggers off labour. It can't only be the size of the babies: if this was so an average mother with twins would start labour when each twin weighed only 3½–4 lbs (when their combined weight equalled that of a single baby).

Other factors that may be responsible for the early onset of labour are the higher level of hormones in a mother's blood. Yet another factor may be the earlier stretching of the cervix, the neck of the womb, due to the pressure from the increased load above.

As prematurity is the most common cause of problems in twin babies the longer the babies can remain in the womb the better, provided of course that they are getting enough nourishment.

Is there anything that a mother or doctor can do to prevent early labour? We know that, in general, a healthy well-nourished mother is less likely to have a premature baby, so diet and rest are important. Some obstetricians believe that a period of several weeks rest in bed, particularly for those in their first pregnancy, may postpone the onset of labour and may also promote the growth of the babies. Others have not been convinced that it makes any difference.

If a mother does have to stay in hospital this can be very disruptive to a family which already has one or more young children – children who will soon have to make difficult adjustments anyway. The time and attention that a mother will be able to give them once the twins arrive is bound to be greatly reduced. To be deprived of their mother for several weeks as a prelude to their arrival may be especially upsetting.

Some argue that if rest is needed it is bound to be more effective in hospital than at home, as the mother will be removed from all domestic responsibilities. In practice, however, this may increase her anxiety. She may be more relaxed if she can supervise the family's life. Even if she cannot do any physical work, there is no reason why she shouldn't plan the daily menus, organise the shopping and the daily school collection rota from her bed – particularly if she has a telephone. But much more valuably, she will be able to give precious time and reassurance to her children: her confinement may actually increase the time she can spend with them.

It must be hoped that the health and social services, as well as self-help groups, will work together to make true bed rest at home feasible. However much extra help a family may need when the homemaker is in bed it is most unlikely to cost anything like the daily rate for a hospital bed. Such considerations might help governments to reappraise present attitudes and policies and provide the necessary services.

Another very common question is, 'If I do go into labour early is there anything that can be done to stop it?' Often there is not. Indeed if the 'waters have broken' most doctors would not wish to delay delivery for longer than two days in case an infection got into the first baby's sac following the breaking of the seal. On the other hand, in its early stages, labour can sometimes be stopped by giving certain drugs such as Ritodrine which reduce the activity of the womb.

Sometimes labour can be stopped and it may not then resume for several weeks – when the babies will be much stronger. Even if delivery can only be postponed for a few days this may make a crucial difference. A steroid drug, such as betamethasone, if given to the mother during these few days can greatly reduce the risk of the babies having breathing problems when they are born. The steroids cross the placenta and stimulate the production of a substance, surfactant, in the babies' lungs.

I have already mentioned that the cervix may start to dilate earlier in a twin pregnancy and this may precipitate labour. Thus it makes sense to try to stop the cervix dilating prematurely. One method is to try to keep it closed with a stitch, often called a Shirodker. Here again, however, obstetric opinions differ about its effectiveness.

Until we learn more about what causes premature labour and therefore how to prevent it, it is vital that premature babies are born where there are doctors and nurses with the special expertise and equipment for looking after very small babies.

Many mothers fear a longer and more painful labour with twins. Some even think that they will have to go through the whole labour again for the second baby. In fact the contractions are usually no more painful nor protracted than in a single pregnancy. A mother may, however, feel more discomfort just because of the heavier weight she is carrying. But many mothers have told me that neither their labour nor their delivery was as difficult as they had expected. A few found that it was actually easier than having a single baby. This may have been because the twin babies were smaller.

Nowadays it has become rather artificial to compare lengths of labour in different sorts of pregnancy as these will depend on the practice of the particular obstetrician. Some accelerate labour after a certain length of time. Others will only do so if the mother or babies are becoming distressed. But in the days when labour just took its course it seems that twin labours did not, in general, last any longer than single ones.

The delivery room

Many parents, if not forewarned, are surprised by the large audience that gathers in the delivery ward. One mother recalled how she felt as if she was 'part of a circus act'. Others fear that such an impressive gathering of doctors and nurses must mean that complications are expected. It is true that some people, such as the anaesthetist, are there only in case they are needed. One or two paediatricians will be there to check that the babies are all right. An obstetrician will be there as well as the midwife if one of the babies is not presenting in the normal vertex (head first) position. But many in the audience will be there to learn. The delivery of twins is a particularly interesting event for any junior midwife or doctor and they have relatively few opportunities to learn the skills required. Someone having their babies in a teaching hospital might expect several medical students to be there too.

Once they are in labour most mothers are so concerned with the babies and their safe delivery that they do not mind how many people are watching. They also realise that doctors and nurses do have to learn. If, however, the size of the audience is upsetting, a mother has every right to ask that it be reduced.

All that really matters to most mothers is that their partner should be there – to give support and encouragement and to greet his babies. Much is said about the importance of early mother-infant bonding but too rarely do we consider the relationship between a father and his newborn babies. With twins it is perhaps especially important that this should develop early.

All hospitals now allow, most encourage, the father to be present during labour and a normal delivery. Some will ask him to leave if, for instance, forceps are needed to deliver the baby. Others are happy for him to stay throughout, even for a caesarean section, as long as it is under epidural anaesthetic (the mother is therefore conscious). It is wise to discover the policy of a particular hospital well ahead. If a couple want to stay together throughout the delivery they should request this, preferably in the antenatal clinic.

Presentation of babies

The great majority of single babies present, and are born, head first: that is in the vertex position. Not so twin babies. It is quite common for one or both of them to come buttocks first – a

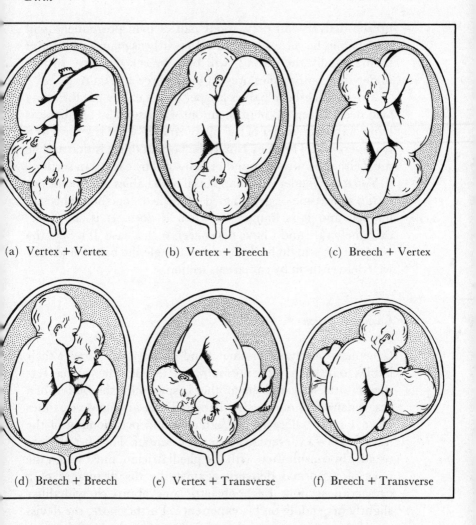

(a) Vertex + Vertex   (b) Vertex + Breech   (c) Breech + Vertex

(d) Breech + Breech   (e) Vertex + Transverse   (f) Breech + Transverse

4/1 Presentations – different positions in which twins may present
for delivery

breech delivery. In only about half of twin pregnancies will both babies be vertex deliveries. In nearly as many cases one of them, usually the second, will be a breech delivery. In just under 10% both babies present by the breech (Figure 4/1).

Most breech-born babies are perfectly healthy but they may well need forceps to help them out. Occasionally one baby is lying across the outlet of the birth canal in what is known as a transverse lie. The baby cannot be born in this position and he must either be turned round or delivered by caesarian section.

You may wonder what happens if both babies try to come out at the same time or get tangled or 'locked' together. This can happen and it is dangerous when it does. It is, however, extremely rare and I have never seen such a case. If it does the obstetrician will do his best to disentangle the babies and may well deliver them by caesarean section.

Caesarean section

Obviously nearly all mothers (and obstetricians) prefer their babies to be born in the normal way – through the vagina. It is the 'natural' way and the mother is spared the discomfort of a scar when she is nursing her babies. There are, however, times when for the safety of the babies – and occasionally of the mother too – a caesarean section is essential. The obstetrician, usually in consultation with the paediatrician, must weigh the risks of a normal delivery against the disadvantages of a caesarean section. Each obstetrician's approach will differ slightly depending on his experience. Furthermore, the devising of new techniques and more accurate methods of checking the unborn babies' health will also affect decisions about when to perform a caesarean section.

Reasons for doing an elective (pre-planned) caesarean section include extreme prematurity, some breech presentations, and a mother's small pelvis in relation to the size of the babies.

Prolonged labour, or the distress of the baby or the mother may demand an emergency operation, that is after the mother has already been in labour for some time. Occasionally the first baby arrives normally and the second has to be delivered by caesarean section either because he is in an awkward position such as a transverse lie or because he is showing signs of distress and immediate delivery is called for.

Pain relief

Even with single births most mothers like to have some pain-killer, an analgesic, during labour. Because of the added discomfort and because of the increased chance of needing forceps nearly all mothers of twins have either analgesics or an epidural injection – a local anaesthetic injected into the base of the spine. Epidural anaesthesia is now becoming increasingly popular and more readily available. It has the advantage that the mother feels no pain whilst remaining fully alert. Should she need a forceps delivery she is already prepared without having to wait for either a local or a general anaesthetic. Thus valuable time can be saved. Even a caesarian section can be safely done under epidural anaesthetic and a mother can then have the pleasure of seeing her baby or babies as they are born and of holding them immediately.

The second baby

Once the first twin has arrived most mothers are so thrilled – and exhausted – that they temporarily feel that they can't face working up to the birth of another. One baby feels quite enough. Luckily the second one usually comes quickly and easily without too much effort on a mother's part. The first baby has prepared the way. Some babies follow straight on and appear only a few minutes after the other. Occasionally if left, the second could take hours, even days. The record interval between two babies is 65 days! (This case was reported in the United States in 1958. One twin, which lived only 15 minutes, weighed 12·8 oz, while the surviving one, a girl, weighed 2 lb 14 oz.) In such an extreme example the mother goes out of labour completely – which is just as well! There indeed may be times when the doctor will actively try to delay the birth of the second baby by labour-inhibiting drugs. One mother who had delivered a very premature twin weighing just 1 lb (which sadly died) did not start again for 4 weeks. By this time the second twin weighed nearly 3 lbs and survived.

But most twins will be born within twenty minutes of each other. After this time the second baby will generally be encouraged on its way if it is showing no sign of coming on its own. All that is usually needed to stimulate labour is the rupturing of the membranes of the amniotic sac. If this fails the womb may again be stimulated with drugs.

Undiagnosed twins

There are still many parts of the world where the majority of twins are not diagnosed until the mother is already in labour or even until after the birth of the first twin. Even in this country there were many units only 20 years ago which failed to detect over half the twin pregnancies. I can well remember the expression on the faces of a couple who were just rejoicing in the birth of their little girl, for whom they had been waiting for many years, when the nurse said, 'I think I can hear another.' The doctor confirmed that there was another heartbeat and within a few minutes Robert was born. The mixture of astonishment, apprehension, joy and/or dismay that such parents feel in the space of a few seconds is difficult for most of us to imagine.

However thrilled parents may be with their bonus child, most wish they had had more warning. Apart from the important practical problems of preparing home, help and equipment for two babies instead of one, it is bound to be a strange experience for parents to have to bond to a baby who they have never even thought about. Many mothers develop a strong attachment to their unborn baby. To have missed out on this may mean that some mothers have real difficulty in bonding to the extra baby especially if the first baby was expected to complete the family. Feelings of rejection towards the second baby are not uncommon and even the most concerned mother may take many months to overcome these feelings. It is important that a mother should realise that she is not alone. Many others have felt the same. One mother wrote, 'I had no idea that I was expecting twins until after the first was born and then sister said, "Oh, there is another one there. You will have to do some more pushing." Well I had the family I wanted, a loving husband, a lovely two-year-old daughter and now a baby son. No I would not push again. I wanted no more. The sister was really angry. She shouted at me. So my second son, Simon, was born. Paul, my first, weighed 6 lbs, Simon weighed 2 lbs 11 oz. I went home the next day and was blissfully happy with my ideal family, one girl, one boy, but having this nagging conscience about the tiny one. After 6 weeks the intrusion came home. The rest was a difficult few years which with the help of my husband's understanding I survived.'

Mothers who do have similar feelings can be greatly helped by talking about them frankly – especially to someone who has been through the same experience. Health visitors and family doctors can often introduce such mothers.

Birth order

There is no doubt that the first twin to be born used to be at an advantage, and not only those few who had a title or estate to inherit. The physical and mental health of a child, indeed his very survival, depended on whether he was the first- or second-born.

The second baby often had a hazardous start to life before the development of modern technology for monitoring the health of the unborn baby and means of accelerating delivery. But things have changed. It is probably still a slight advantage to be the first-born but as obstetric skills continue to improve these advantages will get less and less.

Nowadays there should soon be little medical difference between the twins but psychologically there is sometimes kudos in being the first-born. If this does happen it may help to tell the children about the African tribe which considers the second twin to be superior. This tribe says the first-born is sent ahead to check that the world is ready to receive his more important brother!

Similarly it can be helpful to give the second-born child a name whose initial letter comes earlier in the alphabet. The younger child will then come first at least in alphabetical order.

Identical or fraternal?

Once parents know their babies are all right their next question is often, 'Are they identical?' In fact it is hard, usually impossible, to tell just by looking at newborn babies. Identical twins are often very different sizes and this together with the effects of pressures in the womb may mean that 'identical' twins look surprisingly unalike.

Some experts say that they can tell by looking at fingerprints or shapes of ears. At best, however, these are guides. Comparing the fingerprints of two tiny babies is far from easy and trying to remember the shape of a tiny ear as you run between incubators is not a great deal easier. Some parents may have to wait for up to two years by which time it usually becomes clear as to whether or not the children are identical. Identical twins who have all the same genes tend to grow more alike both in looks and size whereas fraternal do the opposite. Most parents naturally do not want to wait so long for the answer. And fortunately there are other aids to the determination of zygosity – that is whether the twins are identical or fraternal. One of these is the placenta.

Placenta

The placenta of twins has caused interest and confusion not only to parents but to doctors and midwives. Even some obstetric text books give wrong information. As a result of this confusion some parents bring up their twins with firm but false convictions about their zygosity. A mother of indistinguishable four year old boys told me, 'Oh I know they are not identical: the doctor said they had two placentas.' Her doctor had not realised that some identical twins have separate placentas.

Another mother whose two little girls not only looked very different but one had dark hair and the other was fair told me they must be identical because they had one placenta. Almost certainly the two placentas had fused together to form one organ and an inexperienced midwife or doctor had not recognised this.

Perhaps this is a good place to discuss the placenta of twins in general. Not unreasonably many mothers expect the first placenta to follow immediately after the first baby before the second baby is born. In fact this rarely happens. Even when the placentas are completely separate both babies are delivered first.

There are three main types of placenta – separate, fused (two placentas joined together) or single. Which of these a mother has depends on several factors. Firstly, whether or not the twins are identical: if identical, at what stage of development did the fertilised ovum divide and, if there are two placentas, where did the ova become attached or implanted in the womb? If the placentas implant close to each other they may, as they grow, fuse together. What decides where the fertilised ovum (zygote) implants itself is uncertain but it is likely that those ova that come from the same ovary and therefore down the same fallopian tube are more likely to implant close to each other and therefore later, to fuse. The different types of placenta are shown in the diagram (Figure 4/2).

Fraternal twins always have two placentas which may be quite separate or loosely joined by membranes or become fused into one indivisible organ.

Identical twins will have two placentas if the fertilised ovum splits within the first three or four days. After that the placenta and outer membranes (chorion) will have already started to form, so a single organ with one chorion and two amnions (inner sacs) will result. Later still, if the amnion has already formed when the ovum divides the babies will share the same sac. These are monochorionic, monoamniotic twins.

The placenta also affords helpful information on the babies' health and development in the womb. Sometimes one placenta is much larger and the baby it serves is usually heavier as a result of better nourishment. The point at which the umbilical cord is inserted into the placenta can also affect the babies' nourishment, especially if the babies are sharing the same placenta. If one cord is centrally placed and the other only drains from one side the first baby is likely to grow more satisfactorily (Figure 5/2).

Of the two-thirds of identical twins with monochorionic placentas nearly all share their blood circulation in the womb. This is because large blood vessels from the two sides of the

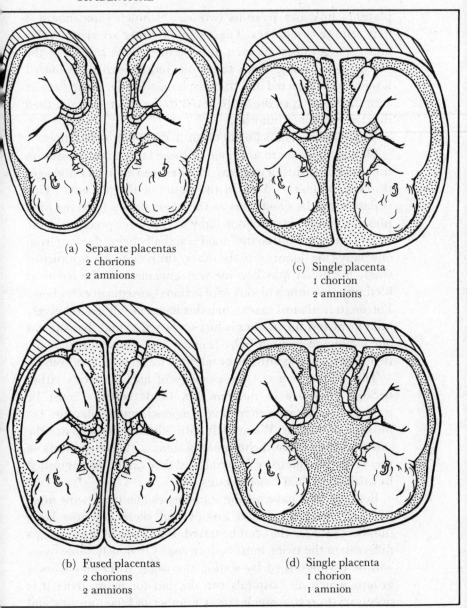

(a) Separate placentas
2 chorions
2 amnions

(c) Single placenta
1 chorion
2 amnions

(b) Fused placentas
2 chorions
2 amnions

(d) Single placenta
1 chorion
1 amnion

4/2 Diagrams showing the types of placenta found in identical and
fraternal twins

placenta link and serve as two-way channels (anastomoses) between the two babies. These may be either arteries or veins and they can often be seen quite easily on the surface of the placenta. To make them stand out more clearly a coloured liquid can be injected into the vessels on one side. It can then be seen flowing across the large vessel to the other side and then into the smaller tributories.

These anastomoses do not occur in dichorionic placentas.

Occasionally there are none of these large anastomoses on the surface but just a one way link between an artery and vein through capillaries deep in the tissue of the placenta. This situation can be dangerous as the blood passes from the high pressure in the artery of one baby to the lower pressure in the vein of the other and so the blood is actually being drained from one baby (the donor) into the other (the recipient). Not surprisingly the donor may become very anaemic and the recipient plethoric (too much blood) with serious consequences for both. Fortunately in most cases when this happens it is in a relatively mild form and the mother is just surprised to find that she has one white and one red baby (Figure 4/3) – it is known as the twin transfusion syndrome or fetofetal transfusion syndrome.

This far we can tell the zygosity of half the twins either because they are of different sex (and therefore must be fraternal) or because they have a monochorionic placenta (so must be identical). We are left with all the pairs who are the same sex and have dichorionic placentas. Three-quarters of these will turn out to be fraternal and they can be distinguished by analysis of their blood groups.

Because they have all the same genes identical twins must have all the same blood groups and there are now large numbers of these that can be tested. If any one of these groups differs then the twins must be fraternal. Obviously some twins will be distinguished by testing the usual ABO and Rhesus groups which all hospitals can do, but for many pairs it is necessary to test a much larger number of blood groups and

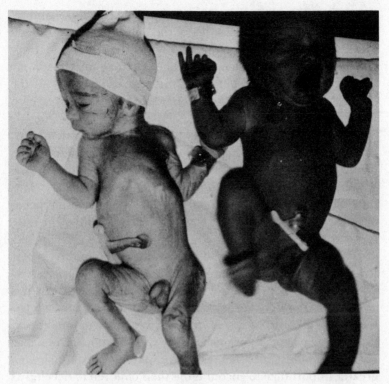

4/3 Newborn identical twins with the twin transfusion syndrome. The donor (left) was anaemic and weighed 3 lbs 8 oz. The recipient weighed 5 lbs 12 oz.

enzymes before a difference is found. If a large enough number are tested then you can be almost sure (about 99%) of the zygosity of a particular pair of twins.

The exact probability can be calculated, and the degree of probability can be increased, if the blood groups of the parents are tested as well. These more complicated tests have to be carried out in special genetics laboratories and cannot, therefore, be available to every family. Nevertheless it is always worth asking that as much as possible should be done to determine the zygosity and, as we have seen, a careful examination of the placenta and testing of the ABO and Rhesus blood groups will provide an answer for a high proportion.

The blood groups can of course be tested at any time in life but the advantage of doing it at the time of birth is that the blood samples can be taken from the veins of the placenta without upsetting the babies.

It used to be thought that the ultimate test for identical twins was the acceptance of a skin graft from the other twin. Apart from the obvious disadvantage that the test would never be done unless medically essential, the supposition is false. It is possible for one twin by chance to have all the same genes necessary to accept a skin graft and still not be identical in other respects.

Having discussed all the possible ways of determining zygosity – why does it matter anyway? That is the question asked by many people – who have not got twins themselves. Clearly it is crucial where twins are later involved in scientific research – and many are at some point in their lives. Much more important, however, most parents simply want to know as much as possible about their babies. Moreover parents may attach even greater importance to encouraging their children to develop as individuals if they know they are identical twins. As they grow up twins themselves are usually curious to know the answer.

It should also be remembered that for those parents considering another pregnancy their chances of having twins again are increased if their twins are fraternal, so this knowledge can affect their decision if and when to increase the size of the family.

Occasionally parents actually prefer not to know the zygosity of their twins and, of course, their wishes must be respected. Equally for those who do want to know every effort should be made to enlighten them.

[5]

Newborn twins

The mother of newborn twins is the focus of great attention and much congratulation and she deserves to be. Sometimes, however, the steady stream of admirers can prove too much of a good thing. A mother feeling the strain of looking after two babies on top of the after-effects of a tiring labour can soon find this well-meant attention overwhelming. A mother should have no qualms in asking that the number of visitors be reduced. It is the babies, not friends, who need her time in these early days.

The emotional, as well as the physical, strain is often much greater for parents of twins than single babies. Many are worried because the babies are small and frail. A higher proportion of twins than single babies are nursed in the Special Care Nursery and those that are very small or premature may need intensive care.

A few Special Care Nurseries have facilities for mothers to stay with their babies but unfortunately these are relatively rare and in most cases the mother has to stay on the general ward away from her baby. It can be very distressing to lie in bed several floors away wondering what is happening to your precious baby when you are longing to have him* in your arms. If he is very ill or if, for some reason, a mother has not seen her baby she may feel desperately lonely and worried. It is then up

* I use 'him' here to refer to either a son or a daughter and shall do so from now on both for the sake of brevity and for ease of distinction from the mother.

to the doctors and nurses to keep her fully informed on the baby's progress.

Parents obviously should spend as much time as they want with their babies. Contact can make all the difference in helping a mother to feel that this is truly her baby and it is usually possible at least to touch a baby however ill or tiny he is. A photograph by her side can also help and it makes it easier to talk about the baby to friends and other mothers on the ward who may otherwise have difficulty in picturing a baby they have yet to see.

Quite often only one baby needs to go to the Special Care Nursery. Should the stronger baby stay with his mother on the general ward or join his twin? There are advantages and disadvantages either way. Some hospitals prefer to keep both babies together. This certainly makes it easier for the mother to give equal attention to both babies. Others feel that if one baby is well enough to be with the mother she should not be deprived of the pleasure of having at least the one baby with her all the time. It is a difficult decision and each case has to be judged individually. If it is decided that the babies should be separated then the mother will need to make a special effort to visit the other one as often as she can.

Mothers with single babies find that one baby is a full time practical and emotional commitment in the first weeks. It is no wonder, therefore, that a mother who has one twin by her side sometimes finds that she is giving all her attention and love to this baby and almost 'forgetting' that she has a second who is equally important. Of course the situation is even worse if one baby has to move to another hospital. This may happen if he needs an operation or more intensive care, such as artificial ventilation.

Sheila, a nineteen-year-old unmarried mother, faced this problem with her twins, Jane and John. Jane was a bouncing 7 lb baby with no problems who stayed by her mother's bed-side in hospital and went home with her after ten days. John weighed only 4 lbs and was so ill that he had to be nursed in the Special Care Nursery for 2 months. During that time Sheila was on her own at home with Jane. She lived a long way from the hospital and she found it very difficult to visit John. And she was so happily and fully occupied with Jane that she scarcely thought about her little boy.

When John finally came home Sheila found that she didn't feel at all the same love for him as she did for Jane. This was not surprising as love usually takes time to develop, but it can nevertheless be distressing. Luckily Sheila admitted to her feelings and was given support by her Health Visitor and by the hospital staff. Gradually her affection for John developed. Other mothers who have more difficulty in recognising this quite understandable problem, or who receive less support, may continue to reject the second child and may even harm him.

It is not unusual for twins to have large differences in their birthweights. Sometimes one baby may weigh more than twice as much as the other. Perhaps surprisingly this happens more often with identical twins. Sarah and Louise are an example (Figure 5/1). Sarah weighed over 7 lbs and Louise under 3½ lbs. It was easy to see why. They shared a placenta but Sarah's umbilical cord through which she got her nourishment was attached to the centre of the placenta whereas Louise's cord was attached right at the edge so that she was receiving nourishment from only a very small part of the placenta (Figure 5/2).

Babies with the twin transfusion syndrome may also be of very different sizes as the donor twin 'gives' some of his nourishment to his twin (Figure 4/3).

It is not only premature babies who go to the Special Care Nursery. Some babies who have had difficult deliveries need special nursing for a while. Others will just be small. About half of all twins weigh less than 5½ lbs, the weight below which many hospitals admit babies automatically to the Special Care

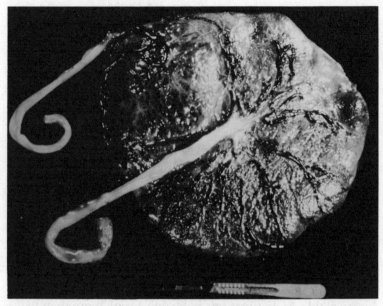

5/1 The placenta of the twins shown in Figure 5/2. The umbilical
cord of the larger twin is centrally placed and receiving blood
from a large area whereas the cord of the smaller one drains
only one small portion

Nursery. Some hospitals are more flexible and will allow babies
over 4½ lbs or so to stay with their mothers as long as they are
feeding well. The decision will partly depend on whether there
are enough nurses to keep a close eye on babies out on the
general maternity ward.

Even when both babies are thriving and stay with their
mother from the start a mother of twins has a special problem in
learning to relate to two babies at the same time. Two babies
who may have very different personalities and needs. If the
babies are difficult to tell apart the problem will be greater –
even fraternal twins can look very alike at first – and it is a great
help if a mother can learn to distinguish between them as soon
as possible. If they have distinctly different clothes and cots

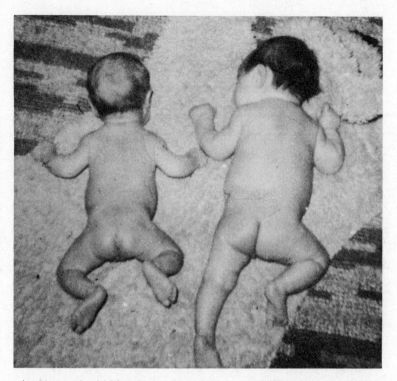

5/2 Six-week-old identical twin girls showing difference in size. At
  birth one weighed 3 lbs 7 oz and the other 7 lbs 4 oz

which can each be identified at a distance, say by colour, this
will help both the parents and the nursing staff to do this. It is
also helpful if people soon learn to refer to them by their names.

Even if a mother can recognise both babies she cannot easily
give either of them her undivided attention. Yet this is vital to
mother-infant bonding. Just as she starts to nurse one baby the
other demands her attention. This is when a father or another
helper can be invaluable. By caring for the crying baby they
allow the mother to concentrate, without fear of distraction, on
the first baby. Dividing attention between babies can be very
frustrating, even guilt-making.

Naming

Plainly the choice of names for a baby is a highly personal matter for the parents. It could be seen as impertinent of outsiders to appear to interfere in it. On the other hand it is as well that parents of twins should think particularly carefully about the implications of landing a child with a 'twin' name for life. Most parents will wish to encourage the children's individuality but they may produce quite the opposite effect if they give the children rhyming names such as Sita and Gita or similar ones like Dean and Darren, Dellis and Dennis or Andrew and Andrea. Similar names for boy and girl pairs, like Robert and Roberta, just add confusion to embarrassment. Incidentally, even giving the same initial can be a disadvantage at school or later with personal correspondence. The best test may be to think what the twins would feel about their names or initials when they have grown up and perhaps become very different individuals.

Feeding

During the first few months the feeding of any baby is the most important and time-consuming occupation for a mother. It will probably be the time when she relates most closely to her baby and it is vital that both mother and baby should find it happy and rewarding.

For a mother of twins it is even more important. Not only does it take up an even larger portion of the day but she will have far less time to nurse them outside feeding times. Provided she has had warning of twins she will have given long thought to what method of feeding will suit her best. How would the many advantages of breast-feeding, for instance, balance against the disadvantages of having to take sole responsibility for every feed? This is obviously a very personal decision and each family

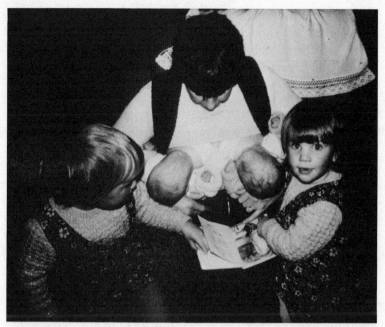

5/3 Mother feeding six-month-old twins and entertaining the two-
and three-year-old sisters at the same time

must work out what will suit them best. The important point is
that there is absolutely no reason why the mother should not
breast-feed if she wants to (Figure 5/3). In the past too many
mothers have been given the impression that it is particularly
difficult or even inadvisable to breast-feed twins. Doctors or
midwives have often been at fault here: some have even positively dissuaded mothers from doing so. Some mothers have
even assumed it would be very difficult, if not impossible, to
breast-feed two babies and no-one enlightened them otherwise.

I have known many mothers who have entirely breast-fed
their twin babies and several have still been breast-feeding
when the children reached their first birthday. As long as a
mother is healthy, has a good diet and plenty to drink she seems
to have a wonderful capacity to provide the amount of milk

needed. Supply equals demand, so to speak. Can a mother really produce enough milk for the optimal growth of her baby? Unfortunately no studies comparing the growth of bottle- and breast-fed twins have been done. This is an important gap which I hope will soon be filled. However, there is nothing to suggest from the many thriving babies I have seen, that breast-fed twins, in general, grow any less well than their bottle-fed counterparts. A mother of triplets has even fully breast-fed her babies.

It is now well recognised that breast milk is the best food for young babies. Not only does it have all the right ingredients but it is easy to digest and it contains antibodies which provide protection against various infections. As twins are more likely to be premature these advantages are perhaps even greater for twins than for single babies. There is, of course, another important factor – cost. Clearly, if a mother is going to breast-feed she will be eating more food and this will cost extra. Research has however shown that this extra food need not be anything like as expensive as the equivalent in powdered milk. A study in the United States has shown that the extra food needed by a breast-feeding mother need cost only a third of that for the milk. Then there is the question of time and energy. Both are in short supply for mothers of twins. Not having to sterilise and make up bottles of milk is a good time saver.

For some mothers the most important advantage of breast-feeding is that it is the one way that a mother can feed and nurse both babies at the same time. Many mothers find that the thing they miss most with twins is the time for nursing and cuddling. At least with breast-feeding you can have physical contact with both babies at once. If the babies are bottle-fed separately the mother can nurse and cuddle as much as she likes but this does take up a lot of the day. Many mothers find they resort to propping both babies against cushions or in bouncing cradles and end up having no physical contact at all during feeds (Figure 5/4).

5/4 Bottle-feeding two babies at the same time makes it difficult to have close physical contact

On the other hand breast-feeding does restrict a mother's freedom. No-one can take over from her however tired she may be and this may be particularly stressful in the middle of the night. Some mothers feel socially inhibited by breast-feeding too. It is much more difficult to discreetly breast feed two babies in public than one. As their social life is often much reduced anyway this can be quite a drawback. We must hope that this particular disadvantage will diminish as society becomes more tolerant of breast-feeding in public.

But even when babies are fed solely on breast milk a mother need not be tied to every feed. Expressed breast milk can be safely stored in the fridge for up to twenty-four hours or in the freezer for several weeks and father can then take over the occasional night feed. Or both parents can enjoy an evening together without worrying about two crying babies and a distraught baby sitter.

Babies who have never had a bottle take time to adjust. They should be introduced to a teat – perhaps with boiled water or orange juice – well before they are left alone with a baby sitter.

For mothers who have decided to breast-feed – how best should they start? They should ask for any available information and, if possible, arrange to see a mother breast-feeding her twins. Care of the nipples before and after delivery is crucial as double sucking on sore nipples can be dishearteningly painful.

It is well known that the sooner after birth that a baby can suckle the greater are the chances of establishing satisfactory breast-feeding. Because twins are more likely to be premature and the mother to have had a tiring delivery, twins are too often whisked away to the Special Care Nursery before they have had time to suckle. If they are very ill or frail then their medical care must plainly override every other consideration but there are many babies who would come to no harm, indeed the opposite, from a few minutes suckling at the breast in the delivery ward. Often a mother can put the first-born to the breast while she awaits the arrival of the second. So all mothers should make it clear to the midwife if they would like to suckle the baby.

The first practical decision is whether to feed the two babies together or separately. There are advantages to both and each mother will decide what suits her best. Unfortunately we do not yet know for certain whether one method is better than the other in promoting a good milk supply. It has been suggested that both babies suckling together increases the production of a milk-stimulating hormone, prolactin, which in turn increases the milk supply. It may therefore be useful to feed them together (at least in the early days) until a good supply has been established. After that the best guide is the mother's comfort.

If the babies are fed separately the mother can concentrate on each baby in turn and may feel generally more comfortable. However, feeding twins will then use up much of the day and the cries of the second hungry baby may be distracting.

In theory it is better to alternate the first feed but in practice the same baby often demands food first. But either way a baby should be offered only one breast at a feed, otherwise the first baby will take the foremilk from both breasts which has a much lower fat content than the hind milk.

The advantage of feeding the babies together is the time saved. In addition, some mothers find that it is actually more comfortable if both their breasts are emptying at the same time. One mother told me she was happier feeding her twin babies than her first single child because the breast that was not being suckled used to feel uncomfortably full. Also the overflow drips were a messy business. There is no need always to feed the babies the same way. Some mothers find that they feed them together when they are busy or when both babies are hungry and at other times enjoy giving attention to each separately.

The position of the two babies while suckling is also a matter of personal preference. An astonishing number of different ones have been devised and none is 'best'. Some of the variations are shown in the pictures (Figure 5/5). Most mothers tend to stick to the same position but some ring the changes.

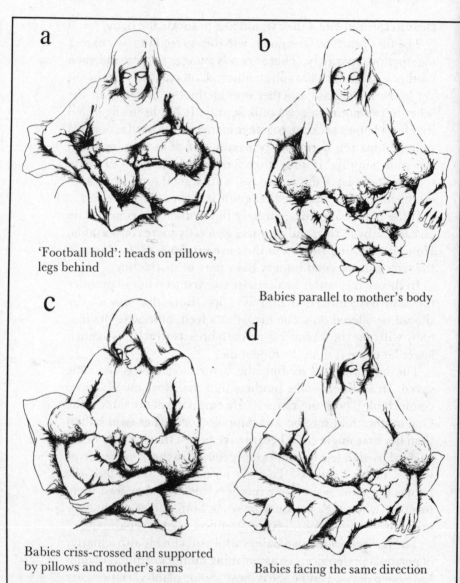

a

'Football hold': heads on pillows,
legs behind

b

Babies parallel to mother's body

c

Babies criss-crossed and supported
by pillows and mother's arms

d

Babies facing the same direction

5/5 Different positions for breastfeeding twins

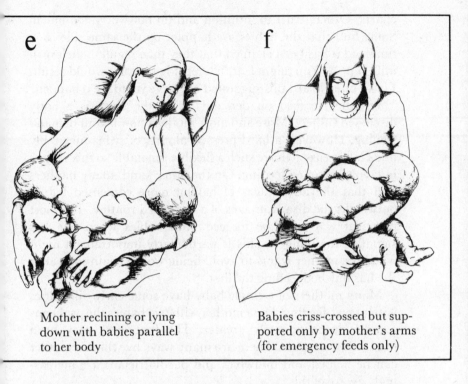

e   Mother reclining or lying down with babies parallel to her body

f   Babies criss-crossed but supported only by mother's arms (for emergency feeds only)

The position of the mother herself while feeding is equally variable. Some prefer to feed from their bed so that they can give themselves the maximum amount of rest and because it feels the most comfortable. The sofa with a supportive cushion for the mother's back and pillows for the babies is also popular. So is the large armchair. A recently produced triangular cushion which was first designed for patients sitting up in bed is an excellent support when reversed (i.e. in front of the mother) for both babies to rest on.

Most mothers prefer to change the sides for each baby at each feed and they have various ingenious methods for remembering who is due for which. A safety pin attached to the bra strap is one favourite. Particularly methodical mothers keep daily charts. Others trust to intuition and do not worry too much. Some find that the babies are happier on the same side each time and it has been claimed that they then regulate their own milk supply. You might fear that lopsided breasts would result. I have often heard this suggested but have yet to see it happen!

Whether to feed on demand or by the clock is a hotly discussed subject. More and more mothers now favour demand feeding. However, a hard-pressed mother of twins inevitably finds it less easy to have such a flexible timetable so this weighs in favour of timed feeding. On the other hand, many mothers find that the advantages of having more contented babies outweighs the disadvantages of a disturbed routine. The most practical way may be to feed both babies when one has signalled his hunger. This is particularly important at night when the mother wants to avoid being woken again soon after she has finished feeding the first.

Many mothers of a single baby have some early difficulties with breast-feeding. For a mother with two babies the problems can be proportionately greater. The first week may be a frustrating struggle. There are many ways by which a mother can be helped and midwives and paediatricians are increasingly aware of this.

The more relaxed and rested a mother is, the better will be her milk flow. Relaxation is a tall order when there are two babies and so the more practical help that she gets the better. No-one can be more useful than a father and he should be encouraged to help from the outset. Trying to feed two babies on your own can be very harassing. At first it is often difficult to keep both babies attached to the breast. If one falls off the other may also be lost while the mother struggles to retrieve the first. If she resorts to feeding them separately her milk supply may be less good and feeding becomes even more time consuming. Until a mother feels completely confident and genuinely wants to be alone it is invaluable to have someone by her side to help handle the babies. Father can be quickly trained in this.

In some pairs of twins, particularly if there is a big difference in size, one may have a much stronger suck than the other. This can, surprisingly enough, be a real advantage to the weaker baby as his twin's stronger suck will stimulate milk production in both breasts.

Some mothers find that the environment of a postnatal ward with its sometimes inflexible timetable discourages breast-feeding. Because breast-feeding initially takes longer than bottle they may resort to the latter in order to conform more easily to the rules of the ward.

Many twins are small so their need for an early supply of milk is greater. A large baby can do without virtually any milk for the first few days but it is crucial for a smaller one to have nourishment from the start. As very few mothers have sufficient breast milk in the first few days it may be essential to give complementary feeds. Some mothers continue to give combined breast and bottle feeds for many months. Others alternate at each feed offering a bottle to one baby and breast to the other. These 'mixed' feeds obviously make more work for the mother but they do give the baby the benefits and pleasure of some breast feeds.

Occasionally a mother chooses to feed one baby entirely by breast and the other by bottle. This may seem to be the babies' own preference or the mother may feel that one is frailer and needs the advantage of the breast milk. In general this seems to be the least satisfactory practice as the mother inevitably spends more time with one baby than the other. But, as with all aspects of breast-feeding, different methods will suit different babies and only the mother can decide.

The first week can be so difficult that many give up breast-feeding at this stage and many others have felt they would have done so if they had not received constant encouragement. It can be vital to have the support of other mothers of twins. When she was six months pregnant Stella, who had breast-fed her first baby, had been to visit Pamela to watch her feeding her five-month-old twins. When Stella's own little boys were born she was determined to breast-feed them. However, the first three weeks were a real struggle. Although James took to the breast fairly well, Jonathan took very little interest. He was always sleepy and seemed actively to dislike the nipple. To add to her problems Stella's breasts were painfully engorged and her nipples sore. She naturally became depressed and told me she would certainly have given up if she had not had daily telephone encouragement from Pamela, assuring her that the struggle would be worth it in the end. For Stella this proved to be true. The problems were soon resolved and she happily breast-fed the babies until they were seven months old. Needless to say she was later a great support to other mothers who were having a similarly difficult time.

Obviously a mother's previous experiences with breast-feeding will influence her decision about the feeding of twins. If she had trouble suckling one she is unlikely to attempt two. In fact, however, I have seen mothers who breast-fed twins more easily than their singletons. Often this is because the approach of the hospital, or the mother herself, was more positive.

Sometimes the very presence of an older sibling may deter a mother from breast-feeding. She may feel that being committed to every feed will reduce the time she can spend with the older child or children. She may also feel that they are being deprived of the chance of playing an important role with the new babies – many children enjoy helping with the bottle feeds. On the other hand some mothers find that breast-feeding allows them to give more attention to the siblings. It takes less time and breast-feeding leaves a hand free to read a story, undo troublesome buttons or whatever. In bottle-feeding both hands are committed. The age and temperament of older brothers and sisters will naturally affect a mother's choice here.

We have discussed the advantages and disadvantages of bottle-feeding. Although it is not possible (unless you have quite exceptionally long arms) to feed and hold both babies together, many mothers hold one while propping up the other on a cushion. A few ingenious mothers devise ways of nursing one baby in their crossed legs and the other in their arms.

It is often tempting to leave one, or both babies feeding on their own – with the bottle, say, supported by a cushion. This practice must be strongly discouraged as there is a real danger of a baby choking.

Preparing the feeds is a time-consuming chore and any safe short cuts should be welcomed. One of these is to make up the whole 24 hour milk supply at the same time. The milk can be made up in a large jug but must then be transferred immediately to the bottles and refrigerated. If it is left in the jug the milk will become more concentrated at the bottom and this can be dangerous. Another time saver is a large plastic bucket or small dustbin which allows all bottles, jugs and teats to be sterilised together.

[6]

The first six months

Apart from winning the pools having twins is about the quickest way to gather friends. People who have never been particularly conspicuous within their neighbourhood suddenly become the focus of attention. Many mothers have told me how their shopping takes twice as long because of all the well-meant but time-consuming remarks of passers-by. Most parents enjoy the kudos and they should. The boost to morale helps to compensate for all the hard work and the sleepless nights.

Sometimes the attentions of strangers can be just too much. Jacky found this when she went shopping with her pretty identical girls. On her way home she always had to pass a long bus queue. She said she would hold her breath and hurry past as quickly as she could: shy by nature she found all the personal remarks, however kindly intended, so embarrassing.

A mother of twins often comes home from hospital thrilled with her babies, encouraged by the general admiration but with little or no idea of what lies ahead. The task can be a shock for those who are not prepared. She not only has to run a home and a family, but has two new babies to look after. Most mothers who have no outside help wonder whether they will ever cope. How will she have time to feed the babies, wash and dress them, wash the mountain of nappies and still clean the house and cook for the rest of the family? And how will she also keep some time for her partner? Most mothers find that a careful assessment of priorities and a set routine are the only answer.

If a mother is to spend as much time as she can with the babies her previous standards of housework are bound to fall. The careful dusting becomes a quick blow around. Cooking becomes simpler and jam- and chutney-making is postponed until next year. Likewise with the babies there may be some things which would have been a pleasure to do for one baby but which are not practical for two. Again, for most mothers, clothes that need ironing are out of the question. So are clothes with fiddly fastenings. A daily bath is certainly not necessary. Babies are quite happy as long as they are regularly topped and tailed.

Susan was a particularly houseproud mother. Her house was beautifully kept and by dint of enormously hard work she maintained high standards despite her young twins. Her furniture and brass shone. There was not a speck of dust. The babies were always dressed immaculately and neatly kept in bouncer chairs or a playpen. Not a thing was out of place, not even the twins.

But by the time the babies reached their first birthday Susan sadly realised she had spent so much time on housework that she had not allowed herself to enjoy the babies – nor they her. She saw that potential and precious cuddling time could never be recovered and wished she had discovered her priorities earlier.

Every mother will, of course, arrange her day differently, depending on her particular circumstances. Father's daily routine and that of older children in the family will influence this and a mother's own energy pattern is important. Some mothers are early morning risers and will do most of their domestic chores before the babies wake. Others prefer the peace of the late evening (if peace there is). The babies' sleeping patterns will also affect plans. Apart from working out the family's own needs a mother will often benefit from the guidance of other mothers of twins who have been through the same planning process.

The inevitably heavy emotional strains of having two babies are easier to face if the physical burdens can be reduced. Many mothers would have saved much exhaustion if they had received more advice on the practical side. Too many mothers still learn by trial and error despite the pleasure other mothers would have in sharing their experience. Unfortunately Health Visitors often do not have much experience of twins – they can offer invaluable guidance to mothers with one baby but rarely to those with two. After all they see a hundred single babies for every pair of twins!

Outings

One of the hardest things for a mother to fit into a busy day is an outing with the children. It is not so much that the twins need the fresh air – they can get that in the garden or on a balcony. The mother needs it. An escape from the house and a chat with friends or neighbours is the best tonic. As one mother put it, 'I feel like a prisoner in the house every day and when I go out I walk everywhere as getting on a bus with twins is a nightmare.'

Some mothers are put off visiting their friends at all regularly by worrying about keeping an eye on two active babies in someone else's precious home. But if she doesn't get out she will not only miss her friends but the boost to morale. It makes a mother feel a lot better. It is good to be told how well one is coping – no-one is more appreciative than a mother who is finding that *one* baby is draining every ounce of her energy.

Life is much easier for families who have a car, although carrying twins safely in a car needs some ingenuity. Clearly all the children must be securely anchored and in the back of the car. One carry-cot can be tied on the back seat and a second on the floor beneath. This allows room for a child car-seat if there is an older child. Otherwise it may be better to remove the back seat.

For the majority who have no car (at least in the daytime), most will prefer to stick to walking with a pram, pushchair or buggy. Buses and trains with two babies (plus pushchair and shopping) are almost impossible. Of the twenty-three mothers I interviewed on this subject only one had taken her twins on a bus on her own during the first year. And she had returned, defeated, by taxi.

Sometimes a mother prefers to have one baby in a sling and the other in a pram. A few carry both in slings, one on the front and one on the back. In other cultures, in Africa and South America, I have seen two babies together on a mother's back looking quite comfortable. I have yet to meet an English mother who carries her twins in this way although one bold mother took her twins and an older brother on a tricycle.

The need to travel is reduced if friends take to popping in. The tactful friend is the one who comes at the right time, stays for as long and no longer than she is wanted and is happy to help with whatever is needed. Others, however, will do the opposite all through and be nothing but a nuisance.

Mothers complain that some visitors expect the job in hand to be dropped so that they can enjoy the twins. If visitors do offer to help it is too often with the feeding rather than the ironing. Sometimes the mother may be delighted to have a break from the babies but more usually she would welcome the chance to take a feed in a more leisurely way knowing that the evening's chore is being done. If you have twins you soon learn who are your really most valuable friends.

Sleep

The survival of a mother's health during the first six months, let alone the happiness of the family, can often depend on whether the twins allow everyone a good night's sleep. One wakeful baby can be disruptive enough: two can destroy the sanity of the strongest mother. Some are wakeful for many months, even years, and this can cause havoc in family life. One mother described her feelings vividly, 'For the first six months I slept in the lounge with the two babies so that my husband could get a decent night's sleep because his work was being affected. In all it was two years before you could really say that they slept through the night, without waking at least a couple of times. Many times I felt as if it would never end – the feelings of desperation were such that I had never imagined.'

The doctor or health visitor who can help with a family's sleeping problems can become their hero. There is, however, rarely a magic answer and most families just have to work out the arrangement that suits them best. The number of rooms available, their positions, the size of the family and the sleeping patterns of the babies themselves will all influence the decision.

Some babies are comforted by being close enough to touch each other. They are better sleeping at opposite ends of one cot in the early months and later having cots near enough so that they can touch each other. If they do wake they will often then resettle on their own. On the other hand many twins disturb each other and if one wakes the second is woken unnecessarily. In this case the cots should be well separated and, where practicable, put in different rooms.

Parents themselves may reinforce troublesome sleeping habits. A mother may rush at the first whimper to comfort one baby so as to prevent the other being disturbed. The children can learn to enjoy this easily-won attention and demand more and more of it. If sleeping separately the wakeful child can be left longer and a vicious circle is avoided.

Parents often assume that twins should be the pair to sleep together even if there is a choice of other brothers or sisters. In fact the twins may sleep better if separated and one or both share a room with an older child. This older child may himself encourage the younger to settle again, or get him to entertain himself, whereas the twin may enjoy multiplying the chaos.

Crying

A crying baby is always distressing to his mother. When conflicting demands prevent her responding to the cry it can be agonising. This often happens with twins and it is difficult, and sometimes impossible, to comfort two babies at the same time.

Should a mother first concentrate all her attention on one baby in the hopes of comforting that one before moving on to the other? Or should she try to console both at the same time? A mother can be torn by this dilemma and the crying may increase as a result of the mounting tension between her and her babies. This situation is particularly difficult if she is in the middle of feeding one when the other cries or if one baby cries consistently more than the other. Should the distressed baby be given more of her time as it seems to be in greater need? Or should she firmly give the same attention to each? There are no golden rules or simple answers on how to manage. Each mother will work out what is best for her. A compromise seems the answer for most.

These are some of the ways that mothers cope with this problem.

Many mothers pick up the noisier baby first. Once he has quietened they can turn to the second baby and concentrate on him without feeling distracted.

Some ingenious mothers manage to comfort two babies at the same time, at least when they are small. One baby over the shoulder and one across the lap is a popular formula. Later, rocking one baby in a 'bouncing cradle' with a foot may comfort him long enough to allow the other a complete feed.

If both babies remain distressed some mothers find they have to temporarily ignore one whilst calming the other. Although this may be the only answer few mothers are happy with it.

It is obviously important that a placid, undemanding baby should still have as much cuddling and attention as possible. On the other hand a baby who is unhappy and therefore feeling insecure will not only take up more time but may actually need it. A baby who is very demanding in the first few months will often become less so later and vice versa. If this happens a mother can then spend more time with the one who was neglected earlier.

The whole problem of relating to two babies at the same time and how this can be done equally and yet individually is one that concerns all mothers both before their twins are born and during the early years. As one mother wrote, 'My biggest worry when they were born was being sure they both had the same amount of love and cuddles. Although I know I love them both as much as each other there was just that niggling feeling . . .'

As twins are two distinct and often very different personalities it is no wonder that some mothers find it difficult to fall in love with both at the same time. Indeed it is surprising that this difficulty is not felt more often than it appears to be. Some mothers may not admit it even to themselves, feeling too guilty perhaps that by doing so they would be failing the less-loved child. We cannot help our feelings, however, only what we do about them.

There is certainly nothing wrong in feeling differently towards the two children. People do. What matters is how we behave towards them. Parents who can enjoy their children as individuals with their own gifts rather than always comparing one with the other will find it much easier to relate closely to both. There will inevitably be times when one baby is much more 'lovable' than the other. Most mothers like a baby who obviously responds to affection and if one baby does this and the other seems to resent or even resist physical contact the mother is likely to feel closer to the first. As time goes on, however, the second baby will develop other means of communication and may be able to show affection in other ways.

Suckling can be another source of tension if one sucks the breast eagerly whereas the other often seems unhappy or puts up a struggle. Sometimes even a short passage of such trouble in the early days can make a big difference to a mother's later feeling about her two children.

If the babies are of very different size at birth a mother will often feel quite differently towards the two. She may be proud of her bigger baby and less attracted to the smaller one. Alternatively she may feel more protective towards, and fonder of, the little one who so needs extra care. A mother may also have unjustifiably different expectations of the two. Even if both are quite healthy parents may expect more of the bigger one, that he should walk sooner, or talk first. Yet these are stages of development that are usually quite unrelated to size.

A father sometimes has more difficulty than a mother in responding to both babies. One father found he continually responded to the baby who was most like himself and was unmoved by the other baby's bids for attention. He sensibly sought help through the Twins Clubs Association on how to cope with the problem.

It is not only parents of twins who have a more complicated process of bonding. So do the twins themselves. They too have competition for their affections. A twin baby develops two strong emotional ties at the same time – one to his mother and one to his twin. When one thinks about it most twins spend more time with each other than they do with their mother, so this can easily become the stronger of the two ties. It is interesting to see how some babies seem acutely aware of each other from a very early age, just a few weeks, whereas others take little notice of their partner for six or seven months. I have also seen pairs where one is obviously intrigued by his brother or sister but is shown no interest whatsoever in return.

[7]

Help

I have yet to meet a mother of twins who did not find the first six months hard work. But some make it even worse than it need be because they fail to seek, to accept or to make the most of outside help. One mother said, 'I felt I would have failed if I could not cope on my own.' Another said, 'I'd be ashamed to see other people cleaning my house.' By failing to use whatever help is offered a mother can actually do a disservice to her babies, to her husband and to her other children. It is always harder to accept help than to give it. For a mother of twins it is especially difficult because she cannot imagine how she will ever be able to repay the debt. But one day she will and in the meantime all useful offers should be accepted.

Father

In most families the father is the most constant helper. Once a father has got over the excitement of having twins the harsh reality may hit him just as hard as his wife. Where he used to enjoy a peaceful breakfast with the morning paper now he has a bottle in one hand and is lucky if he can grab a bit of toast with the other. When he would have been watching *Match of the Day* he is now making up the next day's supply of milk.

Fathers are greatly needed and most respond to the call. Even those who have shown little interest with helping with one baby usually rise to the occasion with two. Most fathers, however, are already working hard outside the home – indeed some may have taken on extra work because of the financial burden of two extra children. It may therefore be unreasonable to expect such fathers to give much help with the babies except at weekends. One father trying to do his best for everyone was up at night comforting babies and then falling asleep at his office desk the next day. Not surprisingly there were complaints from his boss. Careful thought has to be given by both parents to getting as much rest as possible. For instance there is no point in both parents being woken every time a child cries. Some couples find it best to do alternate nights 'on call'. In other families the mother does all night calls during the week and the father those at the weekend. Either way the one off-duty remains relatively undisturbed. Knowing that you are not expected to respond often enables you to be less disturbed by the cries. Of course if the babies are breast-fed the main night-time duties are bound to fall to the mother. In which case father may be able to give mother a 'lie in' in the morning while he gets the rest of the family up and dressed.

Obviously the amount and type of help a father can give will depend on his own working timetable – sometimes the family routine may be altered to fit in with this. With bottle-fed babies for instance, many fathers can help with the early-morning feed and then again with the evening feed on their return from work. Bathtime can be made to coincide with father's 'free' time.

Another major task often undertaken by a father is the shopping. This he may do on his own or he may be part of the whole family outing. Alternatively he may look after the babies whilst a mother gets on unimpeded.

Even the most willing father, especially if these are his first babies, will feel apprehensive about handling very small babies and of course many twins are extremely small. He should, therefore, get as much supervised practice as possible in the early days and the more he can accompany his wife to the antenatal baby care classes the better. In the hospital, particularly if the babies have to spend some weeks in the Special Care Nursery, there will be plenty of opportunity to learn the skills of nappy changing, bathing, feeding and so on (Figure 7/1). If the nursing staff do not invite the father to participate in these activities he should make his interest known to them.

Because of the financial burden imposed by twins parents may seriously have to consider which of them is the most effective money earner. When there are twins rather than a single baby it is even less likely that both parents will be able to work. It is harder to arrange for twins to be looked after by someone else or for them to accompany mother to work. Thus in some families the mother may become the breadwinner and father take on the traditional mothering role. This happened in one family I knew where the mother was a doctor and the father a teacher.

Children

The role of the other children as helpers must not be under-estimated. Yvonne, who was on her own with three children, could not imagine how she would have coped without two-year-old Anne being able and willing to fetch and carry and to entertain the babies. Children like helping as long as their help is appreciated. They will do so willingly provided that at some point in the day they can have their own time when they can have their mother's undivided attention.

Grandparents and friends

For a lucky few, grandmother lives nearby. She can be a great help. A grandmother who is always there when wanted and never when not is a godsend. Occasionally a grandmother will make a full-time commitment to helping with the babies in the

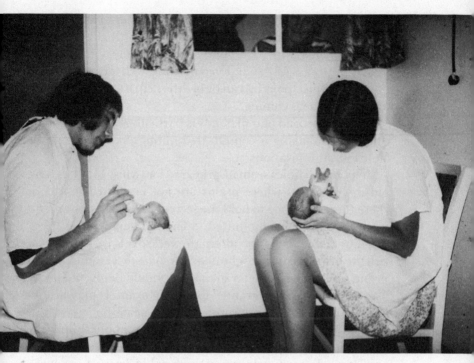

7/1 Fathers should be involved with the care of twins as soon as possible. Parents feeding their premature twins in the Special Care Nursery

early months. She can be a wonderful support. On the other hand she can be overwhelming. Mothers have to remind themselves (and grandmothers!) that it is their home and their babies and that, however well-meant the advice, it is only a mother who can really know what is best for her own family. Few grandmothers will have had experience of twins themselves, so they will not be qualified to give the authoritative advice they might otherwise have offered.

Clearly few grandmothers will be able to help full-time. But some can arrange to come regularly – perhaps to help with the midday feed, for example. Others living further away may come for one day a week – enabling the mother to do her main housework or shopping. However much or little time a grand-mother spends with her family, most mothers find that a regular pattern is essential. Even the most well meaning grand-mother who just 'pops in' can be of little help if a mother doesn't know when she is coming.

A reliable second pair of hands is particularly valuable when a mother is making a complicated outing: like a visit to the clinic for immunisations.

Many baby clinics seem ill-prepared for twins. Mothers have told me of places where prams are not permitted inside; or where there is no-one to hold the second baby whilst the first is being examined or immunised. Some mothers have even re-sorted to taking babies on alternate weeks. It is wise to discuss with the health visitor how best to overcome these difficulties. A certain time may be quieter so that help could be given. Special dispensation might be granted for a twin pram. It may be that there is another, more appropriate, clinic nearby.

All that has been said about grandmother applies similarly, of course, to any close friend. There is no more precious friend than one who can help on a predictable basis. One lucky mother had a rota of friends who came every afternoon during the early months. They prepared the evening meal and, above all, gave her moral support.

Health Visitor

The Health Visitor may become a very close friend to the family in these early months. Every family with young children has a Health Visitor. She is a qualified nurse who has done a special training in the care of young children. She knows not only about their illnesses but also about their health and physical and mental development. She can tell you about the best food for children of different ages and about practical care. She will advise about immunisation and minor illnesses. She will keep a careful eye on the children's development, checking this from time to time. She visits regularly at home and will also be readily available on the telephone. Should you want other guidance, for instance on family allowances or home-helps, she will put you in touch with the appropriate people. Not least she can put parents of twins in touch with each other. A Health Visitor may work directly with your family doctor or she may work with the community health services. Either way there will be a baby clinic where she can talk to mothers, weigh the babies and where a doctor will be available for immunisations, developmental checks and for discussing worries the mother may have.

A Health Visitor may, however, have little experience in the practical and emotional difficulties faced by mothers of twins. Mothers often feel that they are teaching their Health Visitor so a mother may have to cheer herself with the thought that others will benefit in the future from her struggles.

Although your Health Visitor will not have time to give you a lot of practical help, she will advise you on how to find it. In some countries a mother of twins is automatically eligible for the equivalent of a home-help, rightly I believe. In most parts of the UK this is not the case although it varies from area to area. But at least your Health Visitor may be able to support your own case.

But there are other sources of help. Reliable school children can be invaluable, and may also become close friends. There are many sixth forms who allocate an afternoon a week to 'social care'. The students have the choice of visiting people in their homes or in institutions such as nurseries or old people's homes. It is well worth asking around. There could be one, or even two students who would be interested in helping a family with twins. Often there is competition for the task.

Diana, a young mother with lively six-month-old boys, was at her wits' end. She had no help whatsoever and felt trapped in her home. But the thought of going out on her own was just too much. Someone suggested she should contact the local comprehensive school. Two sixteen-year-olds, Susan and Jill, were delighted to adopt the family. To start with they came for one afternoon a week. They did things together with the mother and learnt how to handle the babies. Once they were seen to be reliable they took the boys for walks giving the mother a much needed break. Soon the girls became firm friends of the family and came much more often than their once-weekly allocation. They also became frequent baby sitters.

Student nursery nurses are another group who are often looking for experience with individual families. The principal of such a college is well worth approaching. One mother wrote to the Twins Clubs Association, 'You might like to know that I took up the suggestion in your newsletter to contact an NNEB course and as a result have a charming girl for two weeks from 9–4.30 every day.'

Self-help groups

It is not only practical help, however, that a mother needs. She wants advice and tips on how to cope with a particular situation, what equipment to buy, how best to carry two babies, what to do when one is crying and there is no spare pair of hands. Perhaps most important of all, she needs a sympathetic ear. There is no better person to help than someone who has been through the experience herself – another mother of twins. As one mother of six-month-old twins wrote, 'I have twin sons of six months and a daughter of three and I find the only thing in this area is "Ohs!" and "Ahs!" but nothing of any help . . . just to have someone to understand your delights and exasperations is a great help.' In the past such a mother was often difficult to locate. Many mothers knew no other mother of twins and did not know how to set about finding one.

Over the past few years this has changed. As self-help groups spring up all over the country most areas now have a 'Parents of Twins' club. Usually the address of this is prominently placed in the antenatal clinic. Otherwise the Health Visitor should know the secretary's address. If there is any difficulty in locating the nearest local club the national organisation – the Twins Clubs Association – will be happy to provide the address. If there is no club in a particular area addresses of other mothers of twins who have requested contacts are given. When a few of these mothers have linked up they often decide to start a club themselves. Local clubs are all run according to the needs of their members. Most have a common theme. Parents are welcome to join from the moment they hear they are expecting twins. They meet regularly, usually in the evenings. These meetings may just be for a chat and a cup of coffee with a clothes and equipment swop shop. Others often have visiting speakers. Some also meet in the daytime with their children. Many of them hold large gatherings once or twice a year, for example at Christmas or at a summer party, when all the family is welcome, including grandparents (and great grandparents). Sometimes one or two clubs get together to benefit from each other's experience.

Until the mid 1970s there were only one or two clubs in the whole of the UK. Then there was a sudden increase, and by 1978 there were twelve clubs. Members from these twelve got together and decided to form a national umbrella – the Twins Clubs Association. The idea of this national association was not in any way to reduce the identity of each local club. Each remained autonomous and continued to be run according to the needs of its members. The idea was that the Twins Clubs Association should act as a co-ordinator and should do those things which a local club, because of lack of resources and influence, could not do on its own. In particular, it offers support to parents of twins who have no local club. It will also offer support to parents of triplets or quads (*see* page 173).

Each year the secretary receives many hundreds of letters from parents.

The Twins Clubs Association encourages parents to start clubs by passing on names of other parents in their area and by providing guidelines derived from the experiences of members of established clubs. It soon became clear that a lot of parents had only needed a little encouragement, for within a year over a hundred clubs had started. There are now about 150 clubs in the UK.

The Twins Clubs Association also helps families who have special difficulties, as members of a local club are unlikely to have any experience of such specific problems. One group is for families with twins who have special needs such as mental handicap (*see* page 150); another is for single parents; there is one for families with adopted twins (*see* page 136), and another for those who have lost a twin (*see* page 161). Finally there is the Supertwins Group for parents of triplets or more (*see* page 173). In all these special groups the Twins Clubs Association puts families in touch with each other and with other appropriate self-help organisations.

A way in which the Twins Clubs Association indirectly helps families is by increasing public awareness of the difficulties and needs of families with twins. For instance it persuaded one travel firm to provide a second cot free in the parents' hotel room.

The Twins Clubs Association also tries to enlighten the medical profession. There is a medical and educational group composed of parents who are working or have worked in the medical, caring or educational professions. By meeting regularly to educate themselves they can then go out to teach others.

The Association has regional representatives who act as co-ordinators for all the clubs in their area. They also provide a close link with the Twins Clubs Association committee.

Unfortunately most, but not all, clubs are primarily for mothers of twins although fathers are welcome to some social functions. Fathers, sometimes as much as mothers, welcome the opportunity to share their experiences and so the Twins Clubs Association is hoping to give more support to fathers in the future. It seems that a lack of babysitters is often a bar to both parents attending local clubs together.

There are some mothers who do not wish to join the activities of a club but may greatly welcome an introduction to just one mother of twins. If the club does no more for that mother it may have made a great difference to her happiness particularly during the first year.

[8]

The family

Brothers and sisters

Nearly all older brothers and sisters share the excitement and thrill of the prospect of two babies instead of one. Their joy is not spoiled by apprehension. If there are two children each will be delighted to think he will have his own baby. If there is just one older child then there will be 'a baby for mummy and a baby for me'.

During the pregnancy a child must be encouraged to feel that he will have an important role when the babies arrive and will be greatly needed. He must also be prepared gently for the fact that his mother won't have as much time for him even though she will love him just as much. In fact he often begins to realise that 'his' time will be reduced long before the babies arrive. His mother may first disappear for a rest for a few hours each day at home. Later she may leave him to go into hospital, possibly for several weeks. This may be his first long separation from his mother. Already his delight at the prospect of twins may be beginning to pall.

A child must always be told what is happening and why it is happening, within the limits of his understanding. There is nothing more frightening for a child than the disappearance of his mother to some unknown place. It is a help if he can either accompany her to hospital or visit very soon afterwards so that he knows exactly where she is. It may not be obvious to a child why a pregnant woman goes to the same place as the seriously sick when she is not 'ill'. Photographs can be reassuring reminders to little ones whose memories are short. Whoever is to look after the older child whilst his mother is in hospital not only will want to know him well but also to understand his particular dislikes or fears, as well as any special words he may use. A child's adjustment can be made more easily if the new caretaker (who will often be the father) occasionally takes on the mother's role beforehand, for example in putting the child to bed.

It is as well to get a stock of peaceful occupations for older children early in the pregnancy. A mother who is confined to bed at home will then have things to keep them occupied.

Once the babies have arrived the children are usually proud and enjoy showing them off. This pride may, however, soon turn to jealousy if they find that all attention has been diverted to the babies. It is strange how insensitive friends and even relatives can be. All attention is focussed on the twins and the older child is ignored (Figure 8/1). One mother became so concerned at the way that people ignored her three-year-old that she had a seat specially fitted onto the pushchair pram so that the twins could not be seen until the sister had been acknowledged. Even grandparents sometimes need reminding to greet an older child first before focussing their attention on the babies. A poignant remark came from a six-year-old brother of young twins after the departure of an elderly aunt who had thanked his mother for the 'lovely day' she had had. 'I think it was really the twins that made it such a lovely day for aunty, wasn't it mummy?'

In some families where there is one older child the twins may relate to him as much as they do to each other, but in other families the single child may feel very isolated. His parents are a pair, so are the twins. Both seem to exclude him. The twins may actually do so. The isolation is intensified if the twins have their own language or means of communication which he can neither understand nor enter into.

A child is bound to resent the sudden switch of attention to the new arrivals, particularly if until now he had been the only one and thus the centre of attention. It is important that elder brothers and sisters should feel that they have a new and vital role. They may often enjoy the idea that they are in partnership with mummy as caretakers of the twins.

It is also crucial that an older child knows that some time in the day, however short, is 'his' time – an uninterrupted time when he can have his mother's undivided attention. And equally important, of course, is a time with father. A bedtime story alone with father can often make up for a lot of the frustrations of the day.

Most children, if not all, will sometimes resent the twins but they will also usually be very protective towards them. It is extraordinary what unnecessary anxiety can be caused by thoughtless remarks – joking friends say to the three-year-old 'Which one can *I* have?' and a three-year-old's sense of humour cannot cope with this. The thought of losing a baby put one child into such a state of anxiety that he refused to allow his mother to take the babies for a walk where the threat, as he saw it, might be carried out.

Father

The overwhelming reaction of fathers to the news of twins seems to be one of pride although one father, admittedly fifty years ago, sued his wife for divorce when he heard she was having twins. He thought that two babies must mean two fathers and therefore that she had been unfaithful. Fathers are more enlightened now and many just consider it a sign of superior virility!

Very occasionally a father feels that there is something odd or

8/1 Attention is focussed on the twins and the elder sister is ignored

not quite right about having two babies. Perhaps, as in some primitive cultures, he feels it is animal-like. But fathers with these reservations soon get over it when they see the admiration bestowed on them by friends. One father who for the first few months would not be seen out with the babies was enthusiastically and proudly pushing them around in the pram at every opportunity by the time they were six months old.

Clearly a mother of twins will turn to her partner for help very much more than she would do with a single child and because of this a father is likely to spend proportionately more time with his two children than he would with a single child. It is perhaps not surprising therefore to find that the relationship between a twin and his father may be closer than with a single child. This is one of the compensations for all his hard work!

Nevertheless a father is likely to find the first year a strain. He is almost bound to lose some of his wife's attention and care. She will no longer have time to cook the special treats; to iron his shirts; she may be too tired to enjoy the sex life that they were used to; or even to listen as sympathetically to the problems and frustrations of his day. She just wants to tell him about hers! Her tiredness may make her irritable and arguments may flare up over trivia. He may become jealous of the demanding twins. Because of the financial strain of a larger family he may also have to work longer hours or, more likely, to cut down on the luxuries.

Mother

The feelings of a mother are the most mixed of all. She may swing from pride and joy to guilt or frustration depending on the moment and her tiredness. She may feel all these emotions at the same time. Pride is an overriding and justifiable feeling for nearly all mothers of twins. To cope with two babies at the same time and to come out smiling is indeed an achievement.

On the other hand society expects mothers of twins to rejoice and is surprised when they don't. It is no wonder that mothers of twins often feel guilty. Guilty that they are not enjoying the babies as much as they should do. Guilty that they are not giving them as much love and attention as they had planned or had given their previous child. They may feel guilty about the unequal attention they give to the twins or that they find one of them more lovable than the other.

A mother may also feel guilty about not giving her other children the attention they deserve. She may no longer help them with their homework. She may hurry them through their news of what has been happening at the playgroup or school instead of encouraging them to tell her more. She may be unable to go and hear her daughter in a school concert or watch her son playing in a football match because of the distraction that two toddlers might cause.

She may feel guilty towards her partner not only because she isn't looking after him as she used to but because she is no longer the attractive girl he married. Make-up is now for special occasions only and a visit to the hairdresser is a thing of the past. In addition, two possetting babies have meant that all her best clothes have been put to the back of the wardrobe.

A mother may also feel frustrated with herself: frustrated that she can no longer keep up her previous domestic standards, but frustrated even more that she seems to be losing herself. Every minute of the day seems to be spent looking after the family and home – 'Where is the time for me?' she often wonders. Those who enjoy housework are frustrated to see their standards fall. Those who enjoyed a career outside the home miss the outside stimulation but more worrying, they may fear they will never be able to cope in such a high-powered atmosphere again. One mother, a journalist by profession and an avid reader by nature, found that it was all she could do to concentrate on the newspaper let alone a book during her twins' first year. She was terrified that this intellectual regression would become irreversible and that she might never be able to enjoy intellectual pursuits again. The fear was not justified. Two years later she was happily doing freelance writing again.

A weekly evening class or just a few hours' part-time job can do wonders in cheering one through the next load of dirty nappies.

Those who value their independence may feel demoralised by having to depend so heavily on other people. Often a father has to take time off work (normally using up his annual leave) to accompany his family to a clinic or hospital. Because they are confined to the home or the immediate vicinity mothers become increasingly reliant on their partners which may reduce their self-esteem or strain the relationship.

One of the hardest things for many mothers to cope with is their chronic tiredness in the early months. However tired they may have felt in the past, they always knew that there would soon be a chance to have a good lie in and sleep it off. But with young babies, particularly two, there seems no prospect of being able to have a complete break to catch up with all the lost sleep. If on top of this a mother is feeling frustrated and harassed then her feelings of tiredness increase. A rest is more important to her, and to the rest of the family, than a tidy house. If, instead of doing housework she can have a well-earned rest during the few hours that mother-in-law takes the children off her hands, her time could not be better spent. But most mothers find this difficult and there is no easy answer.

[9]

Identity

We must all have seen pairs of adult twins who behave very much the same and dress alike down to the last detail. They are not only inseparable but seem to enjoy being treated as a single unit – 'the twins'.

Such patterns are usually established in the early years, by children having little encouragement or opportunity to develop as separate individuals.

People are now more aware of the importance of all children, including twins, developing their own individuality from the start. Many parents, however, find it difficult to put their intentions into practice. Social pressures are against them. Many parents who plan to dress their children differently find that this causes such disappointment to grandparents and friends – and anyway they are given so many sets of identical clothes – that they succumb to the pressure and dress them alike after all.

Several parents I have known had seriously planned to start dressing them differently 'later on' but had found they had left it too late. Children get used to looking alike and some resent a change. Many parents who leave this change to the second or third year meet with such vehement opposition that it becomes virtually impossible.

The youngest pair I have heard of who had such troubles were ten months old. When given different clothes for the first

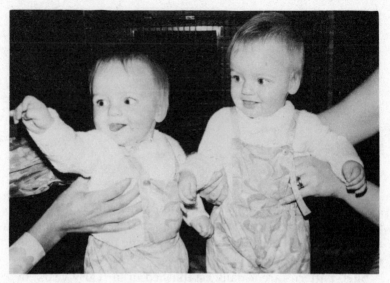

9/1 When dressed alike identical twins are often difficult to tell apart

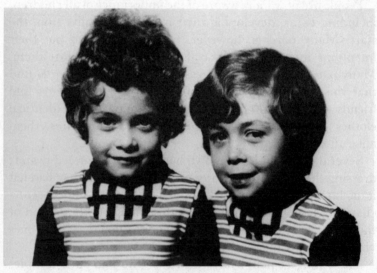

9/2 When the twins look different similar clothes are no problem

9/3 Dressing identical twins in similar styles but different colours
     makes it easier to distinguish them

time they refused to be consoled until they were again dressed
alike.

'Should we dress them alike or not?' – sooner or later most
parents of same-sex twins will ask themselves this question.
Plainly the main issue is nothing to do with clothes. It is one of
identification. Will dressing the twins alike mean they can no
longer be recognised apart? (Figure 9/1). If so, it is probably
best to dress them differently. For fraternal twins who are
unmistakable it matters much less (Figure 9/2).

If, however, they are identical twins and you particularly
want to dress them alike some other means of distinction is
essential – different hairstyles, for instance, or an initial or a
name brooch. Some twins are dressed in the same style but
different colours (Figure 9/3). This method reduces the task
and tension of choosing two outfits but still has the advantage of
distinguishing the children. If they are dressed in identical
clothes the children only have to cross the room unobserved
and most visitors – or baby-sitters – will no longer know which

is which. If, however, they are in different colours they will remain recognisable at least for that visit.

The more alike they are physically, the more important it is that they be distinguishable in other ways. But there are still parents who find this hard to accept. A teacher told me of eleven-year-old twins in her class: one was confident and did well in her school work, the other was diffident and work for her was much more of a struggle. The teacher naturally wanted to approach the two children differently but she couldn't tell them apart. They were always dressed identically, down to the last detail. When the teacher requested that they might have some distinguishing feature, however minor, the mother refused permission – even for one to have a hairslide.

I have met several fathers who still get confused between their teenage daughters. This must be disappointing, even humiliating, for a child who wants to be respected in his or her own right, especially by the parents.

For the many older twins who still dress alike their motives seem various. For some it is just habit; others find their tastes have developed so similarly that they always choose the same clothes. Some feel insecure without a mirror image by their side. I knew one pair of fourteen-year-olds who dressed alike. One was much tidier and more serious than the other and it turned out that this was the twin who insisted on it. Apparently she feared that, left to her own initiative, her sister would look scruffy and then be confused with her.

Grandparents and friends should be encouraged to call the babies by their names right from the start (we have already discussed the advantage of easily distinguishable names). If people have difficulty in recognising each child any distinctive features should be pointed out, and there may often be a place for initialled or discreetly named clothes. Photography is another occasion when there is the temptation to treat twins as a unit, always taking the twins together. Worse still, parents may not afterwards be able to remember which was which because it is often more difficult to distinguish twins in photographs than in real life – a note should always be made at the time. Whenever possible separate photographs should be taken as well: all too often a family has no photographs of the children individually.

Of course what matters even more than physically recognising the children apart is consistently thinking of them as two individuals with their own talents, likes and dislikes, and personalities. Even in the very early weeks a mother can often notice differences in the temperaments of her babies. One may be more active and demanding, the other more contented and placid. Their needs are different and it would be absurd to think of them as a single unit. This becomes increasingly important through the years. Even identical twins will have different natures; they will have different tastes; they will not always feel tired or hungry at the same time; they will not always want to do the same things. Separate outings should be arranged from an early age as not only will it increase the twin child's independence but friendships may develop more easily. Many single children (and some adults too) find it easier to build relationships one to one than one to two.

It is fascinating how some identical twins can have such different personalities and we really have very little idea as to what influences the development of these differences. Clearly it cannot be in their genes because both babies must have the same gene make-up. Thus the influences must be from the environment either before or after they were born – or both. It is likely that some influences do occur in the womb because babies often show their differences very early in life. Also it has been shown that identical twins whose weights were very different when they were born are more likely to have differing personalities than those twins with similar birthweights. The smaller twin is often the more demanding one and perhaps he has every right to be when he has had such an unfair share of nourishment before he was born!

Although the natural individuality of twins, as of all children, should be respected and encouraged there is a danger with some parents of artificially accentuating differences of personality or behaviour. It is inevitable that parents should compare and contrast the behaviour of two children of the same age but sometimes this can lead to an exaggeration of character traits, with the result that they seem abnormal when both types of behaviour – though different – are perfectly normal. Parents may speak of the 'placid' or 'lively' one of their twins and relatives and friends soon learn these stereotypes and perhaps unconsciously respond to each child accordingly. More serious, however, is the fact that children tend to live up to parental expectations of being, for instance, the one who is 'good' or 'naughty', 'quiet' or 'noisy', 'tidy' or 'untidy'. It is important to strike a balance between encouraging and exaggerating differences between twin children. The range of normal behaviour is wide and children vary greatly.

Rosemary, a mother of four, had problems with her twins: Nicola, at two, was a forthcoming, affectionate little girl whereas Simon, her twin, was a shy, timid child. Inevitably grandparents and friends enjoyed the eager responses from Nicola and ignored Simon who was hiding behind his mother's skirt. This only increased the problem, and Rosemary had to remind people to show some interest in Simon however reluctantly he received it.

Another problem about labelling a child with a particular personality is that the parents themselves then expect him to live up to it. One child may be blamed for more misdemeanours than he deserves, whereas the same actions in the other child may pass apparently unnoticed. If parents expect certain behaviour they tend only to notice when the expectation is fulfilled. For instance one mother labelled her children as early as seven months – Ruben, the boy, as naughty and wild and Ruby, the girl, as sweet and easier. A psychologist who was visiting them regularly saw no such obvious differences, yet at the age of two the mother still treated them according to this pattern. She often wrongly suspected Ruben of aggression towards a baby brother but was blind to the several occasions on which Ruby pulled the baby's hair.

Identifying self

We still have a lot to learn about how a child learns to identify his own body image. For twins, particularly identicals, this process must be even more complicated than for a single baby. When most babies are beginning to explore their own bodies, twins may spend as much time in discovering that of their twin. Initially they seem to make no distinction between the two. It is not uncommon to see twins peacefully sucking each other's thumbs. May be it is experiences like the bite of each other's fingers that give the first indication to a baby of the limits of his own body!

If twins are dressed alike the process of identifying themselves may be further delayed. We know that fraternal twins learn to identify their own mirror-images several months before identical twins can. The majority of twins recognise the reflection of their co-twin in a mirror before their own (Figure 9/4). It must be confusing for them. An example of this was shown in five-year-old identical girls who were trying on new dresses. One said to the other, 'Go and stand over there so that I can see what I look like.'

Many twins call themselves by their twin's name and I have often asked three-year-old twins (who have given me their first name) 'What is your other name?' to which they reply with their twin's name rather than their surname. In one pair of identical twins Bert referred to his twin, Bill, as 'other one Bert'.

Finally we have discussed the importance of parents encouraging the individuality of their twin children. Are there any ways in which other people can help? One is by naming them

9/4 Young identical twins find it difficult to distinguish between
their own and their twin's mirror image

correctly, not as 'the twins' nor a duo such as Jill/Jane but each
by their own names. Another way is to allow each to celebrate
separately, for instance having a birthday card and a cake each.
Presents need not necessarily be the same and even if the items
are identical they can be wrapped in different papers.

Only an exceptionally energetic mother will provide separate
birthday parties. But perhaps more important is that each child
should choose the friends he wants to invite.

Pre-school

The pre-school period is highly important for all children: it can have such a lasting effect on their long-term development. For twin children it is particularly critical for this is the time they must try to become independent of each other as well as of their mother. Twins can, of course, enjoy their special relationship but they should not be dependent upon it.

Behaviour

Despite the inevitable rivalries and jealousies of brothers and sisters twins are usually strongly interdependent. They always have each other during times of stress and tend, therefore, to be less dependent on others, not least their mother. Mothers often say that twin children seem to have less need of the approval of their parents and are less responsive to guidance and discipline.

If their parents are cross with them they know that they can always turn to their twin for comfort. This can be disconcerting for a parent when the reprimand given to one is reflected by tears from both. One father, whose twins are now grown up, still remembers, with remorse, an occasion when he smacked his three-year-old son. He suddenly felt the flailing of tiny fists on his back as the tearful twin sister came to her brother's defence.

Sometimes the lack of response to discipline can be very

distressing to a parent and it seems to be particularly common in four-year-old boys.

Some mothers are at their wit's end and are thankful when the children go off to school. The children often behave perfectly well on their own and it is probably best to take advantage of this and to enjoy them separately whenever feasible. For instance it may be possible for them to go to playgroup or nursery at different times, say one in the mornings and the other in the afternoons.

The same remedies can be tried if the children fight a lot as in the case of these four-year-old fraternal boys. Their mother writes, '. . . individually they are both great fun to be with, both very strong characters, very affectionate but so different in temperament. However, when they are together I am in despair. They fight *constantly*. If I play a game, usually they stop. But if I have to leave them to answer the 'phone, for example, they are off again. . . . If they play without squabbling for ten minutes in any one day then I feel I've done well. When I have one twin alone I have a wonderful time – it's like being with another person.'

Within a pair one twin may be the dominant one. Sometimes it may be the same one throughout life but quite often twins switch in leadership from time to time. Sometimes it depends on the circumstances. One twin may be the more physically adventurous whereas the other may be more socially confident. This is not a cause for concern unless one twin dominates to such an extent that the other is unable to express himself. In school medical examinations I have often found one child will reply to all my questions regardless of to whom they are addressed. If I then see the same children separately the previously silent one will usually answer perfectly readily. However, if a pattern becomes too firmly established the retiring one's school progress may be seriously held back.

Development

Many people are under the impression that twins tend to be small and backward. In fact the great majority of twins will be of normal size and normal intelligence. Indeed it is remarkable how quickly most twins catch up considering how small many of them are when they are born.

It is true that some studies have shown twins to be slightly smaller, on average, than both single children and single adults. Likewise the average intelligence quotient of twins may be a few points lower than that of single children.

Whether it is being a twin that gives these people a slight disadvantage, or whether it is the problems that go with being a twin (such as prematurity and low birthweight), is not certain. It would, however, seem that being a twin is at least partly responsible for the differences. One of the reasons for thinking this is that if one twin dies at or soon after birth the single survivor tends to do better than twins who are brought up in a pair. Furthermore it is known that brothers and sisters who are born very close together are at an intellectual disadvantage and twinship is the extreme example of close spacing.

One study of eleven-year-olds showed that where singletons in general scored 7 points higher in IQ testing than twins, siblings born close together were superior to twins by only 3 points.

Before parents of twins become disheartened by these statistics they should realise that large studies give figures for the average child. The range for individuals is enormous and there have been many brilliant as well as successful twins.

Those who start slowly may give unnecessary worry to their parents as many catch up later. Neil and Jonathan were an example. Neil weighed 6 lbs 10 oz when he was born and Jonathan 4 lbs 12 oz. Jonathan was a difficult baby and slow to feed. He gradually, however, caught up with his brother.

When they started school, both were very slow to read and to

grasp number concepts. This was despite lots of encouragement at home. Now, at 15, they are taking their 'O' levels a year
ahead of most of their contemporaries. One is an avid reader of
the Financial Times and the other has just built himself a
go-kart.

Few studies have distinguished between identical and non-
identical twins but where they have it has been shown, not
surprisingly, that identical twins are more similar in their
mental development than fraternal. Identical twins become
increasingly alike with age and tend to have spurts and lags at
the same time. Fraternal twins become less alike and eventually
develop no more similarly than two brothers or sisters.

It is always interesting to see what happens to twins who
were of very different weight to start with. Sometimes the
smaller one catches up amazingly. James and Stuart were such
a pair (Figure 10/1). James weighed 3 lbs 8 oz when he was
born, Stuart weighed 5 lb 12 oz (Figure 4/3). But by eighteen
months there was only 5 oz difference between them and when
they were eight years old James was actually half an inch taller
than Stuart. On the other hand Louise and Sarah, who weighed
7 lbs 4 oz and 3 lbs 7 oz (Figures 5/1) kept these differences and
Sarah never caught up (Figure 10/2). They were both healthy
little girls of similar abilities. Louise was sturdy and of average
height whereas Sarah was wiry and petite.

Both these pairs were identical twins so it is mysterious why
the outcome for each should have been so different. It may be
related to the length of time that the smaller baby had been
short of nourishment. Perhaps James had been short only for
the last few weeks of pregnancy, by which time he had already
acquired the potential to grow well. Whereas Sarah may have
been getting less nourishment right from the start so she never
developed the potential to grow as well as Louise. So when
twins are born of very different size we are so far unable to
predict with any certainty whether or not the smaller one will
catch up with his twin.

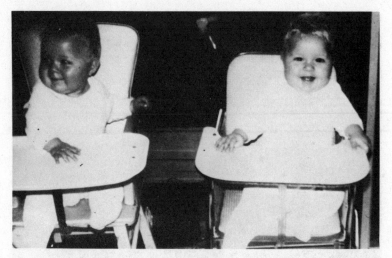

10/1 Some smaller born twins catch up quickly. Identical twin boys shown in Fig. 4/3

(a) at 8 months (smaller born on right)
(b) at 8 years (smaller born on left)

10/2 Some smaller born twins remain smaller. Identical twin girls
      shown in Fig. 5/2 at 7 years. The smaller born is 3 inches
      shorter and 10 lbs lighter

Language

One aspect of development where twins have definitely shown
some delay compared with single children is in speech. Many
twin children whose overall intelligence is normal show significant delay in acquiring language. One study for instance
found that at the age of four years twin children were six months
behind singletons in their language. Another study which
carefully distinguished between several aspects of language
development found that twins were behind in all areas except
one, speed of reaction to speech. Perhaps the constant presence
of another child competing to communicate may stimulate the
development of this particular skill.

There are many reasons why twins may be slow in their speech development. Firstly their mother is likely to be busier and to have less time to talk to the babies and it has been shown that parents of twins not only talk less to their children but they also tend to use shorter and grammatically less complicated sentences. Secondly twins have less need to use the conventional form of communication, language, as they have so many other means of relating to each other. Furthermore twins have a much more difficult environment in which to learn to talk. From the very start twins face problems of communication. There is the almost constant presence of three potential participants – the mother and two children – in any act of communication. There are always two people who receive and two who can respond to any message within the threesome. The children have to learn the process of engaging and disengaging in discourse in a much more complicated way than one child alone with his mother.

Many mothers mistakenly think that twins have less need of attention because they entertain and comfort each other. It has been shown that mothers are less responsive to the distress or demands of twin children, which is not surprising when they are likely to have twice the calls on them. They also give fewer commands, suggestions and in particular explanations.

The most encouraging finding in recent studies is that this speech delay is not inevitable. Twins can catch up if they are given enough help and individual attention. One pair of four-year-old boys was completely unruly, only said a few recognisable words and had a language of their own so were thought mentally retarded. They were driving their mother to distraction. However, with guidance she learnt to give them individual attention and encouraged them to play with other children. Within a year they were speaking fluently and their intelligence quotient had climbed to well above average.

In short, there is no reason why twins should not speak perfectly well. But it is important that parents should try to talk to their children as much as possible even if this is a tall order for tired and busy parents.

Twin 'secret' language

Much has been made of the 'secret' language of twins – a language incomprehensible to others and sometimes known as cryptophasia or idioglossia. There is no doubt that many young twins have special forms of communication but most outgrow it well before they start school and there is little evidence that it interferes with their normal speech development.

There have been isolated reports of five-year-old twins who have no language other than their own but this is extremely rare and only occurs when children have been deprived of normal communication with other people.

Left- or right-handedness

Between the ages of two and three years most children will show whether they are going to be right- or left-handed. Some may be several years older before this becomes clear and others will remain ambidextrous.

Twins are probably slightly more likely to be left-handed than single children, although this is not nearly so common as it was thought. However, it does seem that a higher proportion of twins have mixed laterality, that is they do not have the same sided preference for all three of eye, hand and foot.

As with laterality there is still much confusion about mirror-imaging in twins. It is often said that identical twins can be mirror-images of each other, which means that they have opposite sided superficial features such as birthmarks and hair whorls, or that internal organs such as heart and liver may be reversed and the twins have opposite handedness. It has been thought that this lateral asymmetry or mirror-imaging might arise if the embryo divided late when the left and right sides have already been determined. However, there is no concrete evidence for mirror-imaging and some workers feel that its very existence is in doubt.

Illness

Illness, except perhaps in the first three months, is no more common in twins than single children. But when they do succumb it is likely to cause more disruption to the family as the chances are that one will follow the other. It is also difficult if one child has to go into hospital. This can be very distressing for both children – not only are they separated from each other, often for the first time, but one or other will also be parted from his mother. If the admission to hospital is unexpected then there will not even be time to prepare the children for this separation. In these cases it is often best for the healthy twin and the mother to be admitted as well. However, there are still many hospitals who are reluctant to admit children for 'social' reasons. In such cases the healthy twin should at least be allowed to spend the day there.

It is not unusual for both twins to be waiting for an operation, such as removal of tonsils, at the same time. When this arises many people would assume that twins should be admitted together. Some parents, however, feel that it is better for the children to go in separately so that they can give each child special attention when he most needs it. Just as it can be disappointing to share celebrations perhaps it is also disappointing to share illnesses and the sympathy that goes with them.

Occasionally hospital staff are blind to the particular difficulties of a mother with twins. One such mother who was breast-feeding her three-month-old babies was faced with a dilemma when the little girl was admitted to hospital for an operation on her foot. The little boy was not allowed into the hospital so the mother had an exhausting time rushing the five miles between the two babies trying to feed them both. Not surprisingly her milk supply suffered.

Even the most well-meaning people can be strangely thoughtless. A surgeon for instance offered a circumcision to a healthy twin just because his brother needed one!

There are no figures available on the accident rate in twins but it would be surprising if it was not higher than average. It is very difficult to keep an eye on two active toddlers or crawlers, neither of whom has any sense of danger, going in opposite directions. Worse than this is the terrifying daring of a bold child encouraged by another, or two of them competing in daring.

Brothers and sisters, let alone single children, rarely get into the same predicaments. In most pairs there is usually an older child with some sense of reality or a younger one who is physically unable to tackle the project. With twins the combination of mutual encouragement and physical co-operation results in far more reckless feats – or attempts.

Twins also engage in pranks which neither child would have the patience or ingenuity to do on his own. One mother described how her eighteen-month-old girls took her purse containing £100 from a drawer and tore each note into small pieces. Fitting them together again was no joke.

There is an added danger for identical twins. If they are dressed alike, particularly in outdoor clothing, many parents cannot tell them apart (Figure 10/3). If a child is about to chase a ball across a busy road a failure to call the correct name can be disastrous.

Not all injuries will be accidental. Even the best mothers and fathers may at times be so infuriated and frustrated by their children as to want to hit them. Many mothers fear that they may reach the end of their tether and actually do so. A very few

10/3 Identical twins indistinguishable in their outdoor clothes

will. It is known that non-accidental injury (battered baby syndrome or child abuse as it is otherwise known) is more common in families under emotional or financial stress. It would not, therefore, be surprising to find a much higher incidence of such abuse in families with twins but it is reassuring to find that this does not seem to be the case.

Figures from the National Society for Prevention of Cruelty to Children show that there seems to be no higher incidence of this kind of injury amongst twins and this is a great credit to parents. Possibly the presence of a second baby offers the mother a diversion in moments of extreme exasperation with the first.

There are, however, times when even the most caring mother is tested beyond her endurance and only with help and support may disaster then be avoided.

Marion had such problems. Her twin boys were born 12 weeks early and each weighed only 2 lbs. They were much-wanted babies and their parents went through agonies for the first month as they watched them struggling for their lives. They survived and at the age of three months they were taken home with much rejoicing to join their eighteen-month-old sister. But they cried almost incessantly for the next two months by which time the poor mother, despite excellent support from her husband, was so exhausted and desperate that she begged not to be left alone because she feared that she might harm the babies. Fortunately she frankly admitted to these feelings. She was then given round-the-clock support and within a few months things were much better and the much-loved little boys have thrived.

In different circumstances with less support and greater financial strain this mother might easily have harmed her babies. In fact she has since given great support and understanding to other parents living through similar crises.

The important thing to remember is that many mothers, perhaps most, feel desperate at some time or another and if only they can call for help, help will be given and after a much needed rest the mother will probably feel quite differently towards her children.

[11]

School

Starting school is a significant milestone for any child. Both parents and children talk and think about it a lot before the big day comes. When the children are twins the parents will necessarily have to consider a number of other aspects. They must decide whether children should be in the same class or even in the same school. Perhaps they should start together and be separated later. If so at what stage? There are no simple or universal answers to these questions and the advantages and disadvantages will have to be weighed for each pair, indeed for each individual child, within the limits of what a particular education authority can offer.

You might expect that teachers would be the best advisors to the parents. It is surprising, however, how many teachers have given little thought to the special problems of twins or have rigid ideas which do not allow for the special needs of each child. For instance some teachers assume that twins must always stay together regardless of their relationship with each other or of their individual abilities.

By the time a child reaches secondary school many twins will themselves choose how they want to be placed.

Before deciding on different schools, however, parents (and the twins) will have to consider carefully the implications to the family. Holiday times may differ, as may general rules and uniform requirements. There will be twice as many sports days, speech days, concerts, etc., for parents but the non-participating twin will rarely be able to go to them.

It is in the early years that the parents may find it hard to decide if, when and how much the children should be separated. The prime advantage of separation is that the child can more easily develop his own talents and personality. Constant comparisons with his twin are avoided and he will be less likely to have particular personality traits emphasised just because they are different from his twin's.

Some twins are used to performing exactly the same as each other and like it. They may actually strive to get similar results. Thus the brighter child under-achieves while the slower one may be put under undue stress. On the other hand it may be that when one twin is more able than the other the second one just 'gives up'. For instance if one is a star cricketer and the other average the second may not bother to play at all. Had the children been in different classes or schools the second would probably have been happy to join in with the others. The less talented twin may not give himself the chance to develop fully in many kinds of school activities.

Girls tend to develop faster than boys in the early years. This sometimes causes problems in girl/boy pairs. The girl often tends to 'mother' the boy. He may enjoy this but it may harm his relationship with other children, not least the boys.

Some twins are very dependent on each other. Obviously some degree of mutual support is beneficial. There are few scenes more heart-warming than a five-year-old rushing to comfort her sister when she falls in the playground or a little boy hurrying to his twin's defence when attacked by a larger child. However, if they are over-dependent on each other they are prevented from making other friendships. Likewise if the dependency is all one way one twin becomes spokesman and performer for both.

There comes a time when a child likes to have part of his life independent of his parents – he may want to keep it entirely to himself. If the twins are constantly together at school, one may repeatedly report what has happened to the other (whether good or bad) and this may be distressing to the one being denied his important right to privacy.

We must also consider the needs of the school or class. Sometimes twins can become too much of a good thing. They combine forces and become a powerful unit. They can disrupt a meeting or cause chaos in a class. If so it is better that they are separated, both for their own sake and for that of the rest of the class. The same applies if one twin tends to constantly distract the other.

Many twins use their twinship to confuse the teachers and to entertain the other children. This is harmless fun in small doses but it can become too easy an attention-seeking device. Much more often, however, it is the teachers and other children who are careless and do not make any effort to distinguish the twins. Praise or blame may be given to either or both indiscriminately.

If the children are in the same class the differences are readily seen and parents may become unnecessarily anxious about their progress. All children vary not only in their rates of progress but also in the periods in which they are progressing rapidly and the times when they go more slowly. Parents may be worried by these differences in performance and these differences will be more obvious if both children are in the same class. One child may be racing through the reading books and the other taking them more slowly but it should not be assumed that the second is failing.

There are, of course, advantages in the twins being together at least for the first year or so. On the whole they will have less trouble settling into school than single children, probably because they are reassured by the presence of their twin and feel less vulnerable. They have lost their mother but still have each other.

There is, therefore, much to be said for letting them start in the same class at least for the first term. Certainly if the twins are so dependent on each other that they pine and do not join in school activities if they are parted, there is no point in forcing a separation. Usually this only arises in twins who have never been separated before. If this is the case any separation must be arranged as a very gradual process. The first stage may be for the two to sit at different tables within the same class, or at a different table at meal times and then progress from there.

If twins start in the same class the timing of the later separation must be carefully planned. It is better if they separate when a change is due anyway. Otherwise one will remain in a familiar environment and the other may feel rejected as he sets off alone into the unknown. Some schools may be flexible enough to allow the children to move when it seems in their own best interest. Others may have a more rigid policy and insist that changes only take place at certain stages in the school's life. It is important that parents talk to teachers beforehand to find out the policy of that particular school. It may even influence their choice of school.

Teachers' attitudes

Many teachers welcome the arrival of twins and are eager to accept advice from parents as to how best they may help the children to cope with their twinship at school. Others, as I have said, still have set and often false ideas about twins. They expect them to be slower than other children, to look alike and to like being treated alike. Many teachers assume they will not be able to tell the twins apart and therefore make little effort to do so. Even more worrying, they assume they will have the same abilities and personalities.

On the other hand they may go too far the other way and constantly compare and contrast the behaviour and achievements of the two children. With siblings this can cause enough distress, but with twins it can be even more damaging.

A leaflet, designed for teachers, *Twins at School* has been produced by the Twins Clubs Association. This can be useful as a basis for discussion between parents and teaching staff.

Preparation

Twins, like any children, need long and careful preparation for school. They need particular help learning to be independent of each other. The more they are used to doing things on their own the easier will the transition be. Some mothers find that it is helpful if they get used to going to at least one playgroup or nursery session on their own. Jane, for instance, sent Thomas and Jonathan, her identical twins, together to playgroup on one morning and on the other two mornings one or the other went on his own. This increased their independence and also gave them time with their mother's undivided attention.

It is not only the twins who need to be prepared for school – so does the mother, especially if there are no younger children. Suddenly her fully-occupied (and noisy) day is transformed into six hours of peace. Initially this may seem bliss; long overdue curtains are made, letters are written, the bathroom is decorated. But very soon a mother may feel the vacuum. Many mothers of single children have told me how bereft they felt, even lonely, when the last child started school. With twins a mother's feelings may be even more extreme. Mothers need to plan carefully how best they will adapt to this new pattern of life.

Starting school

If the children are starting in separate classes it is often helpful if a friend or relative can come to school with the mother until the children are settled. Otherwise a mother may feel torn if both children are tearful and she has to leave one comfortless.

For twins who are not used to being separated the first weeks are bound to be difficult. It is important that the teachers realise the problems and ensure that the children see each other at intervals through the day – for instance they could sit together at meals.

If the children are in the same class it is important that the teacher and the other children can easily tell which is which. In identical twins different hairstyles as well as different clothes are helpful. If the children are in uniform then initials or decorative name brooches are useful. If the school is divided into houses and the twins are placed in different ones the badges or ties can be a useful distinction. It is relatively easy to remember, for instance, that Ruth wears red and Yvonne yellow.

Children, like adults, are fascinated by twins and most twins find themselves warmly welcomed by their school-mates. They usually have no trouble in making friends. They have the advantage of being used to sharing and to communal activities.

Many twins will have different friends from their co-twin and this should be encouraged. Inevitably one child, particularly if he is more outgoing, may make friends more easily than his twin. There is no way of preventing this but it is important that the less gregarious one should have his interests and pleasures respected and that he is not just automatically swept up by the group surrounding his twin.

12

Adoption

Amongst the several thousand children adopted in England and Wales each year a number will be twins. It would not be surprising if the proportion of twins was higher than in the general population, as there must be single mothers who are prepared to undertake the heavy responsibility of bringing one child up on their own but who are overwhelmed by the thought of two.

In the past twins were often adopted singly but it is now generally agreed, particularly by parents of twins, that if possible they should be placed together. Fortunately there are plenty of couples eager to adopt two babies and most, if not all, healthy twins will be adopted together. We know very little about the relationship that develops between twins before they are born but it is almost certainly there, as is demonstrated by the loss felt by a surviving twin whose twin dies at birth (*see* page 162). Furthermore, it is likely that many adopted children find it sad to have no known (blood) relations. Twins adopted together can greatly enhance each other's sense of security and it would seem wrong to deprive them of this unnecessarily.

A problem arises of course if a mother, or indeed a family, feels that she can cope with one baby but not two and therefore wants the second adopted. Is it fair to separate the twins, especially as one is likely to feel that the other had been chosen in preference to him and that he himself had been rejected?

If such a situation does arise the natural mother will need

careful counselling so that she becomes aware of and can give deep thought to the long-term implications of such a decision. She must realise that the adopted child will be told of his background, including his twinship. Adoption agencies now give adoptive parents quite a lot of information and they encourage full explanations to the child when he seems ready for it. At eighteen he will himself have access to his birth record.

If the mother still wishes a baby to be adopted, a welcoming adoptive home will almost certainly be a happier environment for the child than that of a rejecting natural family. Many people however would feel that in such cases it would be better for both babies to be adopted (together).

A similar problem arises if one twin is ill or handicapped. Should both babies still be adopted together? Is it fair to jeopardise the chances of adoption of the healthy child, for the sake of the twin? Should a child be burdened with a handicapped twin if it can be avoided? Although there are many people ready to adopt a single child or even a healthy pair of twins, handicapped babies are much harder to place. Despite all these disadvantages many people feel that keeping the twins together is the least harmful alternative. Apart from the other considerations a healthy twin may sooner or later feel guilty for having 'deserted' his needy twin. Fortunately there have been an increasing number of couples ready to adopt handicapped children, so there is now a good chance that a satisfactory home can be found for both babies together. If a handicapped child is not placed with his twin it may still be possible to maintain some contact. Some adopters are now happy for their children to maintain contact with certain relatives.

In such cases the healthy twin will often be ready to go to the adoptive parents sooner than his twin. The handicapped baby may need longer in hospital if, for example, he has had an operation, or if he is having difficulty with feeding. When this situation arises there need be no delay in placing the normal baby and the other twin can follow as soon as he is fit enough.

When a couple considers adopting twins they obviously need very special counselling. In addition to all the information and guidance that all adopting parents want they will be concerned about the special needs of twins. It is important that they should be made aware of the emotional and physical demands of two babies. Like the Health Visitor, the social worker may have had little experience with twins. Prospective parents would be well-advised to contact other mothers of twins and especially those who have adopted them. The Twins Clubs Association has a special group for parents of adopted twins and members of this group are happy to be in touch with social workers and with prospective parents.

Adopting parents may, like most people, underrate the difficulties of caring for two babies and may only think of the obvious pleasures. They are likely to have waited for a family for a long time and like the idea of 'two for the price of one'. Prospective parents need to make sure that it is not the superficial attraction of twins that is the reason for adopting them, and that they have a realistic idea of what it will entail.

As with single babies the sooner that twins can go to their adoptive parents the better. Nowadays some babies can be adopted as 'direct placements' which means that the prospective mother will take the babies straight home from the maternity hospital. She will usually go and stay in the hospital from the second or third day after the babies are born. This gives her a chance to learn about the practical care of the babies and, as a bonus, she has the chance to talk to and learn from more experienced mothers.

Recently a number of adoptive mothers have breast-fed their single babies. Even a mother who has never been pregnant can produce milk – sometimes enough to completely nourish her baby, and at least enough to give both the baby and herself pleasure. The very sucking of the nipple by the baby stimulates the production of hormones which, in turn, cause secretion of milk in the breast. There is no reason why twins should not be fed in the same way although obviously the mother would need a great deal of help as it would inevitably take a lot of time and patience.

Separated twins

Because in the past twins were quite often adopted separately there are many people today who still do not realise they have a twin. Every year more twins discover and meet each other. The reunions are exciting and usually happy.

For instance Jean and Jean first met when they were 55 and have now become known as Jean 1 and Jean 2. When they were born their mother was on her own and she felt that she couldn't manage two children, so she kept the first born and the second was adopted. Jean 1 knew that she had been born a twin but thought that her sister had died soon after birth. Jean 2 knew that she had been adopted but had no idea that she was a twin. It was only as an adult when she became curious to know more about her origins that she discovered in the Registry of Births that someone with the same (unusual) surname had been born within a few minutes of herself. She concluded she must be a twin. After a few fruitless attempts to trace her twin she gave up. Many years later she saw a television programme about separated twins who had been reunited. The programme introduced a social worker, John Stroud, who had a particular interest in separated twins and had linked many pairs. Jean 2 got in touch with Mr Stroud and within a few weeks he had tracked down Jean 1. Both sisters were married and had teenage families. Jean 2's husband, although understanding about her wish to trace her twin, was apprehensive – partly because he feared his wife might be disappointed in the person she discovered, and partly because he feared it might affect their own happy relationship. But Jean 1 and Jean 2 did meet. They had talked beforehand on the 'phone and learnt much about each other. Jean 2 had always assumed that they would be identical twins but when they met they discovered that they did not look at all alike and their personalities were very different. Jean 2 was the talkative extrovert one and Jean 1 the quieter and more reserved. Nevertheless a close friendship developed which they both value deeply.

There have been many similar happy reunions. A few, not surprisingly, are less happy. Children who have been brought up in different social backgrounds may find they are on different wavelengths. Perhaps the most extreme example was a pair of identical German twins, one of whom was brought up as a Jew and the other as a Nazi.

There have been many stories of the extraordinary similarities in taste, interests and dress of twins who have not met since babyhood. There are frequent stories of middle-aged women dressed in almost identical clothes; of women who have married husbands of the same name and have named their children similarly. Stories of reunited twins is a book in itself and the whole fascinating subject of telepathy and extrasensory perception is beyond the scope of this book.

Useful address:

British Agencies for Adoption and Fostering (BAAF), 11 Southwark Street, London SE1 1RQ.

13

The twin with special needs

Most twins are as healthy as single children. A few, however, will have some form of handicap which may be physical or mental or a combination of both. For instance, a child with cerebral palsy will always be physically handicapped, but may well be of normal or even high intelligence.

Handicaps of both types are slightly more common amongst twins than single children. This is mainly because a substantial proportion of handicaps are due to brain damage occurring at birth or in the immediately following weeks and (as discussed in Chapter 4) newborn twins are more vulnerable to this than single babies. For the same reason there is a greater risk of handicap to the second-born than to the first-born.

With the continuing improvement in obstetric and paediatric care, however, any slight difference between twins and single children has been steadily decreasing.

This chapter is primarily intended for parents of children with some disability or handicap but there may be some points which are relevant to families whose twins, though both perfectly normal, are of very different mental and/or physical ability.

Discovering

There is no painless way for parents to discover that their child will be handicapped, but some ways are more painful than others. Uncertainty is agonising, and is made worse if the parents feel that something is being hidden when, for instance, the doctor is plainly worried about the child's progress but continues to say that all is well.

Sometimes the doctor will be uncertain too. He or she may be worried about the baby's progress or behaviour but know that he may turn out to be quite normal after a few months. Premature babies, or those who have been very ill at the start, often cause concern in this way. It may be genuinely difficult for a doctor to know how much of his anxiety – which may later turn out to be unjustified – to share with the parents.

Equally upsetting is a doctor's unwillingness to take a parent's worry seriously. If a mother, for instance, thinks that her child is deaf investigations must continue until either deafness is confirmed or until the mother *as well* as the doctor is happy that his hearing is normal. If parents are not satisfied they should always ask for another assessment or, if necessary, a second opinion.

Sometimes only one parent, usually the mother, suspects that something is wrong. She may find it difficult to share these fears with her partner. It is then vital that there is someone, such as a health visitor, in whom she can confide.

The suspicions of a mother of twins may be roused earlier than usual. This is because when there is a 'normal' model at hand the delayed development of a child is obvious whereas a mother with one child, particularly her first, may not recognise any undue slowness. Comparisons can, however, lead to false worries. A mother brought her fifteen-month-old daughter to see me because she was worried that she could not walk on her own. Her brother had taken his first steps at ten months. The little boy was a sturdy active child: the little girl was placid and enjoyed quietly playing with her toys. Both were well within the normal range but they were just different children.

Some abnormalities will be recognisable at birth. Some, such as a cleft palate or 'hare' lip, will be completely remediable.

Others such as Down's Syndrome (mongolism), which are due
to abnormalities of the chromosomes or genes, cannot be cured.
The long-term outlook in other cases will depend on the
severity of the abnormality. A small spina bifida, for example,
can be operated on soon after birth and the child will be able to
live a perfectly normal life. A more extensive defect in the spine
cannot, however, be fully corrected and the child will be
handicapped to a greater or lesser extent throughout life.

If the problem is apparent at birth, as with Down's Syndrome, parents should certainly be told. If at all possible, they
should be told together, partly so they can support each other
but also to ensure there is no misunderstanding. Most people
when shocked hear only the one cruel basic fact. The long and
detailed explanation that follows is often entirely lost. Doctors
do realise this and parents should never be embarrassed to ask
the same questions as often as they want. What matters is that
they feel that all their questions have been fully discussed.
Unfortunately these questions cannot always be fully
answered. The cause of many handicaps is still not known.

If one twin has a problem parents will inevitably fear for the
other – even if the twins are not identical. Parents should ask for
the second child to be examined by a paediatrician so that these
fears can be allayed as soon as possible.

Reactions

Most people react to the news of their child's handicap as if it
were a bereavement. It is, indeed, a sort of bereavement as
parents have lost the child they dreamed of. They may feel the
same shock, disbelief, numbness, anger and guilt as they would
if their child had died.

Acceptance will gradually come but the parents of a handicapped child have a special difficulty. Whereas death cannot
easily be denied, handicap can be – at least initially. Many

parents take months, even years, to acknowledge that their child is not normal. Others go on hoping for a 'miracle cure' or that their child will 'catch up' later. These feelings are very understandable and parents should try to talk openly about their expectations, their hopes and their fears even if some of them may be irrational – especially so in that case.

It is often difficult for a parent to know who to talk to. They will meet very many people while their child is being initially assessed and some of them may appear to be giving conflicting information. Whom should they believe? It is usually best for a parent to link closely to one person who can assimilate all the information and sort out any confusions. This person will usually be the paediatrician but it will also depend on the child's particular problem and the person to whom the parents find it most easy to relate.

Most children with a problem will be seen at the local Child Development Centre where a team of people work closely together. Although each has a particular speciality they will be concerned with the child as a person and with his whole family.

The paediatrician assesses the child and co-ordinates his overall care. Various therapists help the child and guide the parents in different ways. The physiotherapist is concerned with teaching the child to use his body and helps him to relax if he is too stiff or how best to use his muscles if they are weak.

The occupational therapist guides the parents and child through problems of daily living. Through the imaginative use of aids in feeding, dressing and play, she can help the child to develop his full potential abilities.

The speech therapist is largely concerned with speech but also helps with feeding and swallowing difficulties.

The audiologist checks the hearing and the ophthalmologist the eyesight.

The psychologist will assess the child's intelligence and general abilities and offer advice on any specific difficulties including behaviour problems. Parents of a sick or handicapped child often wonder how much discipline to give. One mother of three-year-old twins, both with cerebral palsy, wrote, 'I feel very guilty a lot of the time especially if they have been naughty and had a smack. You feel torn between telling them off and protecting them.' But a handicapped child has the same ability to test his will against his parents' control as a normal child. Over-indulgence may well make him feel insecure and unhappy. Furthermore if a healthy twin is treated quite differently he is certain to become jealous and resentful. Psychologists can offer advice on how to manage this situation. It is better to seek guidance early, before bad habits are established.

The social worker is also an essential member of the team. She will advise not only on the special allowances and benefits available to families with handicapped children but on the effects the handicap may have on the whole family. Who will look after the other children when the mother brings one for treatment? What about transport? What practical help does the mother have? Has she been introduced to other families whose similar experiences would be valuable to her? Are there financial hardships? (A mother may now be unable to take the part-time job she otherwise wanted.) The social worker will be happy to help with all these and other aspects of the new situation.

Other medical specialists will be involved if the child has a special problem such as a heart defect. The family may also have close contact with nurses, special teachers as well as the Health Visitor and family doctor. This array of professional people can be confusing for parents so it is vital that the team works closely together for the welfare of the whole family. And that very much includes the other twin. There is sometimes a danger that the price of intensive help for the handicapped child may be a disturbed or neglected twin. The 'team' has to be as aware of this as the parents.

Both handicapped

Having a handicapped child is always very sad but if both children are handicapped the family, especially the mother, has an enormous physical and emotional burden.

Stephanie found this with her twins, Jeremy and Rebecca. They were born prematurely and although all seemed well for the first few months it was obvious by six months that something was wrong. Neither of the children was learning to do things as quickly as he should. Jeremy felt very stiff and could not hold his head up properly. A visit to the paediatrician confirmed that both children had cerebral palsy and were going to be spastic.

From then on Stephanie had to take Jeremy and Rebecca on a regular round of hospital visits and treatment sessions. Stephanie was taught to do physiotherapy and this had to be performed on both children several times a day. Because of their stiffness the twins were also difficult to carry, to wash and to dress and Stephanie's whole day was taken up looking after them. Even by night there was no peace as one or other of them would be restless and life was exhausting. The marriage was strained.

By the time the twins were three they were quite big children; Rebecca could now sit up on her own but Jeremy could not, and both still needed carrying. On top of this physical strain was the disappointment and longing for the children that might have been.

For several years Stephanie and her husband had wanted children and were thrilled when they had heard it was to be twins. The marriage has survived but their dreams are shattered because these children, much as they love them, will always need enormous help and the family will never be able to enjoy so many things that other families take for granted.

Often a mother feels frustrated that she is unable to give the children the attention she knows they need. Camilla had this

problem with her identical twin boys. When they were eleven
months old it was realised that they were both profoundly deaf.
This was later found to be due to a rubella (German Measles)
infection that Camilla had caught during the early part of her
pregnancy. The children were otherwise lively normal children
and they were given hearing aids. A special teacher visited
them each week and they had regular speech therapy.

Camilla was advised to spend as much time as possible
talking to the children individually so that each could see her
face and learn to lip read. With two lively toddlers, a four-year-
old sister and a house to run this was extremely difficult. It was
all she could do to keep an eye on the twins and have very
occasional face to face conversations with them. Initially she
felt desperate. But she was sensible (and brave) enough to seek
help.

Family and friends gradually rallied round and somehow she
was soon managing to give each child some time alone with her
every day. Now at five they are doing remarkably well and both
can carry on a good conversation.

One handicapped twin

If, as is more likely, one twin is handicapped and the other
normal the mother has to share her attention between two
young children with very different needs. The handicapped one
is bound to take up a great deal of her time often at the expense
of the normal one.

Marjorie found this a real problem. She already had three
children when she learned that twins were on the way. At first
she was horrified that an already unplanned pregnancy was in
fact two but she soon adjusted to the idea and, with the rest of
the family, eagerly awaited the arrival of the babies.

Her first baby was born – a lusty 7½ lb boy, Jason. When the
second baby, Dean, came there was silence. He did not cry or

move and Marjorie thought he was dead. The doctors gave him oxygen and put him on a ventilator to help him to breathe.

For the first few days it was touch and go whether he would survive. He did so but as the weeks went by it became increasingly apparent that he was not normal. He was stiff and cried a lot. He was another case of cerebral palsy and to make matters worse he had frequent fits. His mother found these terrifying and she never knew when they might happen. Each time she thought he was going to die.

To start with, Marjorie was shattered. What had the doctors done wrong? What had she done wrong? Sometimes she felt angry, sometimes guilty, often both. When Dean's endless crying wore her down she wished he had died at birth. Then the little handicapped baby began to respond to her and she began to love him. When he had the first of his many chest infections she nursed him with all possible care and love.

Meanwhile Jason was thriving – a happy chuckling baby with whom Marjorie would have loved to spend more time. She was torn between the two, but only she could cope with Dean. No-one else could feed him. So inevitably the rest of the family looked after Jason while she attended to Dean.

Dean had regular visits to the hospital to see the paediatrician, physiotherapist and speech therapist. Transport was a problem. She had no one to leave Jason with. It was difficult to cope with him and at the same time to concentrate on Dean. As the children grew their needs became more and more different. While Dean's demands and behaviour were those of a baby (and a very heavy one too) Jason became a lively two-year-old who enjoyed playing with other children.

They were identical twins. By now Dean's handicap had distorted his features but there were still many similarities between the two and these only increased their parents' sadness as they realised how Dean might have been.

The handicapped twin

Anyone with an abnormality, however minor, must go through the process of learning to accept it. A handicapped twin may find this often painful process harder than most people. He can see what he could – or should – have been like. And why should he be the one to suffer and have all the humiliation? These feelings may be particularly painful for the child of normal intelligence with a severe physical handicap.

By the age of five or so both children will be wondering and asking why they are so different. Usually it is best to give the truthful answer, if known, but in terms they can understand.

Sarah first asked when she was seven. She was a second-born twin who had been paralysed on her right side since birth. One night when her mother came up to read a bedtime story she asked why she was different from her healthy sister, Rachel. Her mother explained about her difficult birth and how this had harmed the part of her brain that controlled the movements on the right side of her body (cerebral palsy). Sarah was obviously fascinated by this and has since asked many questions and taken pride in explaining it all to her friends.

One problem is that of celebrating the achievements of the handicapped child in their own right. The first steps of Sarah at the age of three were a much greater achievement than those of her normal twin sister at thirteen months. The handicapped child should be encouraged to feel this. It can help if some activities – for instance riding or typing – are attempted only by the disabled child. The success can then be acknowedged as hers alone.

The healthy twin

The healthy twin, of course, shares the burden of the handicapped child. Both practically and emotionally he will take part of the strain. He will also make all sorts of indirect sacrifices, especially attention. Some healthy twins have a happy relationship with their less fortunate partner; they may support and protect him and offer a great deal of encouragement and stimulation. This should obviously be welcomed and encouraged. The normal child should not, however, feel tied to his twin at the sacrifice of his own interests and friends. By the same token, the parents should make some time, however little, really to concentrate on his interests. This will enrich his life and reduce the risk of life-long unconscious resentment towards his attention-consuming twin.

The feelings of the survivor whose twin has died are discussed in the next chapter, but many of these feelings are shared by a child who has a handicapped twin. He has 'lost' a normal twin. He may well feel guilty about the other's handicap, guilty that he has been the lucky one. He may feel he is normal at the other's expense, by being the first-born or by getting an unfair share of nourishment in the womb. He may be angry with his mother for 'allowing' it all to happen or angry with his twin for causing such an upset in the family. He may be jealous of the unequal amount of attention given to the other child. Sometimes quite severe behaviour disturbances may develop.

Rachel was an example. She was the elder of non-identical twins and there were no other children. Her sister, Sarah, had been an undiagnosed twin and had difficulty in breathing when she was born. Their mother took the babies regularly to see the paediatrician but it was not until they were fifteen months old that she was told that Sarah had cerebral palsy. This came as a blow to their mother but not as a surprise: she had realised how slow Sarah was compared with Rachel.

Intensive treatment followed and each visit involved a 30-mile round trip. Rachel came too as there was no one with whom to leave her, but all attention at the Child Development Centre was naturally focussed on Sarah. Rachel got bored and became bitterly resentful of her twin. Even at the age of two

Sarah still had to be carried and helped with feeding – Rachel resented this too. Also despite the cerebral palsy, Sarah was a warm, attractive little girl of normal intelligence and so it was not surprising that friends and visitors tended to prefer playing with her.

At five Rachel went to the local primary school and Sarah went by taxi to the unit for physically handicapped children 15 miles away. This she enjoyed, in particular the riding and swimming. Both of these Rachel would have enjoyed too and was jealous of what she saw as Sarah's 'treats'.

Rachel's behaviour at home now became increasingly difficult. Sometimes she was withdrawn, at other times she would have temper tantrums and screaming attacks. One day she was suddenly unable to move her right arm and leg. Her parents were terrified that she might have had a stroke. In fact she was unconsciously imitating her sister to attract similar attention. With help from a child psychiatrist she lost the 'paralysis' but she continues to need a lot of help and understanding. Fortunately her parents had sought help and the whole family worked together to help Rachel accept her difficult situation.

Twinship

Most parents are proud of having twins and many children enjoy being a twin. It is often difficult for parents to know how much to promote this twinship when, because of a handicap, the children are different not only in appearance but in the physical or mental age at which they are functioning.

Even with normal twins one may appear physically or mentally 'older' than the other. With handicapped twins the difference may seem to be several years. In such cases it may be embarrassing and harmful to the slower one to dwell on the twinship.

The children themselves should be allowed to be the guides.

If they like to be thought of as twins there is no problem. But others will prefer to be thought of just as brothers and sisters and their wish should be respected.

Dressing the children alike may only serve to emphasise differences – and the same clothes are unlikely to suit very different children. One adult twin whose severely deformed, identical spastic twin had been dressed the same as himself recalled that looking at his brother was like looking in a distorting mirror. He saw a caricature of himself. So, no doubt, did other people.

As discussed in Chapter 9, it is sometimes very difficult to change an early practice. Even if one baby is obviously not normal it may seem quite appropriate to dress the two babies alike but once this pattern has become established it may be hard to change later.

The desire to dress twins alike can go to extreme lengths. One mother with two-year-old identical girls, one of whom was spastic, actually resisted the physiotherapist's suggestion of special boots on the grounds that the two children would have different footwear.

Help

Parents of a handicapped child may feel especially isolated. They may be physically isolated – because it is more difficult to get out – but worse may be the social isolation. They cannot join in the same activities as their friends with normal children. It may indeed be too painful to be surrounded by lots of normal children. These are strange feelings and it is no wonder that parents of handicapped children often welcome the chance to meet others with similar experiences. It may be a great help to meet others with twins and to hear how they cope with the special problem of two children of the same age with such different needs. There are many different self-help groups each concerned with a special problem – for instance the Down's Association, or the Spastics Society, or Mencap (for the mentally handicapped). In addition the Twins Clubs Association is happy to put parents in touch with each other and a confidential register is kept of all families wishing to be involved who have one or both twins with special problems or needs.

Useful address:

Association for Parents of Handicapped Children
8 Lonsdale, Wellington,
    Leamington Spa, Warwickshire.

[14]

The loss of a twin

Few parents of twins, fortunately, will need to read this chapter, although most of them will want to understand the special difficulties of those who lose a twin. Such parents will nearly always continue to think of the survivor as a twin and of themselves as parents of twins.

Losing a child is a tragedy. The tragedy is no less because the parents happen to have another child of the same age. Other people may not realise this, especially if the twin dies at birth. His parents will in fact have additional problems: they will have the difficulty of celebrating the life of one while simultaneously mourning the death of the other; they will not only have a constant reminder in the survivor of the child they have lost but they will also have to help the survivor come to terms with the loss of his twin.

Parents also have to cope with a society which finds it difficult to acknowledge death, especially in a young person, and will consistently avoid the subject whenever possible. With twins such avoidance is easier than with one child. It is possible to concentrate on the living baby and never mention the dead one. This can be very hurtful but so can remarks like, 'Well, two would have been an awful handful,' or 'I don't know how you would have coped with both.' Even doctors and nurses occasionally come out with such thoughtless cruelties.

If one baby is stillborn it is usually the second to be delivered. By the time he is born the mother may have had the first (live) baby in her arms. She will be tired and may hardly notice the birth of the second baby let alone that it is dead. Not, that is, at the time. The midwife and doctor sometimes take advantage of her distraction and whisk the dead baby away without her seeing it and may refer only briefly to the lost baby, concentrating on the healthy one. Their intentions are kind, to reduce the mother's grief, but in the long term their action may have the opposite effect. Because the mother does not experience the full loss at the time, she will feel it all the more deeply later and possibly for longer.

To some parents the idea of seeing and holding a dead baby may seem morbid. But those who have lost a baby nearly always find that contact is helpful and it should be encouraged. After the death of an older child there are many memories and visual images to treasure but with a stillbirth there will be no such memories, however close the mother has felt to the baby for the months before birth. For those who have never seen their lost baby imagining what he might have been like can be very painful. And with twins it is particularly difficult for a mother to distinguish a baby she has never seen from the live baby in her arms. One mother who had never seen her stillborn twin told me she felt that the survivor was 'only half a baby'. Some mothers find themselves wondering what the dead baby looked like almost every time they look at the live one.

Unless they have seen and held the dead baby, mothers of twins may come to think of the double pregnancy as a fantasy. If the mother has not been able to see the baby it can be helpful for her to have a photograph (even an x-ray or ultrasound photograph) just to prove to herself that the nebulous baby really did exist. Naming the baby can also help her to remember him as a real person and to distinguish him from his twin. For many parents it is also helpful to have a memorable funeral service and an individual grave or memorial for their baby.

Many parents like to know whether the twins were identical or not and the doctor should be able to tell this either from the placenta or from blood tests. This is particularly useful if the baby that died had some sort of abnormality. Knowing the zygosity will help the paediatrician or geneticist to calculate the risk, if any, of future children having the same abnormality.

From the moment twins are diagnosed a mother, and father, have been a focus of admiration. In the course of a few hours all this changes. It is an immense let-down. It is not only a blow to parents but to their relatives and friends. It is a disappointment also to the midwives and doctors who have been sharing the eager anticipation. Instead of admitting this disappointment too many people try to avoid the subject or deny the reality of the second baby.

One mother who lost a twin was bitterly hurt when a midwife she had known particularly well in the antenatal ward didn't visit her once after the births. Another mother described how a midwife came to admire her healthy baby and never mentioned the stillborn twin and yet afterwards was seen by other mothers to be in tears over it. Had she not heard about this she might never have known the midwife had cared at all.

The almost exaggerated attention to the healthy baby with no reference to the dead one can be very hurtful. The mother longs to talk about the dead baby but whenever she tries she may meet obstacles designed to distract her away from this baby and focus her attention on the healthy baby. She may take less and less interest in this baby. 'Oh yes, he's all right, but the other one is dead and I want to talk and tell you about him,' was the heartfelt feeling of one mother.

Parents are bound to have endless questions about how and why it happened: a mother may blame first herself and then her doctors and midwives; she may feel guilty or angry or both; she will keep thinking about her lost baby and imagining what he would have been like. She may want to share these feelings and thoughts and if she is discouraged it will be much harder for her to grieve properly – in fact the whole mourning process may be suppressed.

The need to talk will last months, maybe years. A sympathetic listener is invaluable. A bereaved parent should not worry about imposing upon them; their sympathetic ear and support can be crucial and one day the bereaved parents will be able to help others in the same way.

Parents will also want repeated reassurance and, often, explanations. The health visitor or family doctor should be best placed to help, although some questions may better be put to the hospital specialists such as the obstetrician or paediatrician. It is important to ask these questions direct and candidly. Doctors often hesitate to mention a dead baby unless the opening is offered by the parents.

Many mothers are worried by what they experience as a total inner preoccupation with a dead baby. They may feel no interest for the beautiful healthy baby in their arms. Repeated efforts by the midwife to focus the mother's attention on the live baby may only serve to increase a mother's alienation towards him.

It is necessary for a mother to come to terms with her dead baby before she can really relate to and love the survivor. A mother should be reassured that her feelings are quite normal: it is only when she has fully mourned her dead baby that she can wholly concentrate on, even truly love, the live one. As time passes she will feel much more able to cope with her own feelings and memories.

If one baby dies while the mother is still in hospital her feelings in many ways will be very similar to those who have had a stillbirth. In addition, however, she will have gone through an agonising period of uncertainty as the little one fought for his life in the Special Care Nursery. During this time she may have been torn between caring for the healthy baby by her side and visiting the sick one. She may have been encouraged to concentrate on the healthy one, particularly if the other was expected to die. A mother may later regret this as every mother wants to do as much for any baby of hers as she possibly can. If his life is to be short then it is all the more important that she gives him her love and attention while she can. However sick he is she should be able to at least see and touch him. This will also give her more substantial memories.

It is often thought that the arrival of a new baby will usefully distract a mother from excessive grief but a pregnancy following too soon after any stillbirth can be hard for a mother to cope with in that she may have difficulty in distinguishing this new child from his dead brother or sister. Twins are an extreme example of this. A mother experiences the joy of a new life and the tragedy of death at the same time. She is likely to suppress her grief, and relatives and friends often encourage her to do so. It may work for a time but is likely to cause her more suffering in the long run.

It can be difficult in the ward too. A mother with a healthy surviving twin appears just the same as all the other mothers. They too have one baby. They are rejoicing but she is sad as her thoughts are on the dead child. She needs to grieve. It may be that she feels too inhibited to do this in hospital and it is only when she returns home that she can really express her feelings.

Many mothers want to leave hospital as quickly as possible but some are reluctant to do so feeling that they have not completed what they went in there to do: to have twins. They have left something behind. Going home with one baby seems like the final recognition that the other baby will never be. Most mothers feel a terrible sense of failure. They have failed themselves, their partners, their relatives and their friends. Congratulations on the birth of one child can seem hollow when you have lost the other half of the pregnancy. Facing friends and neighbours is bound to be an ordeal, especially those who come up full of expectation, 'You've had them – what are they?' The explanation causes confusion and embarrassment.